降 击 神 通
AVATAR
THE LAST AIRBENDER™

Created by
Bryan Konietzko
Michael Dante DiMartino

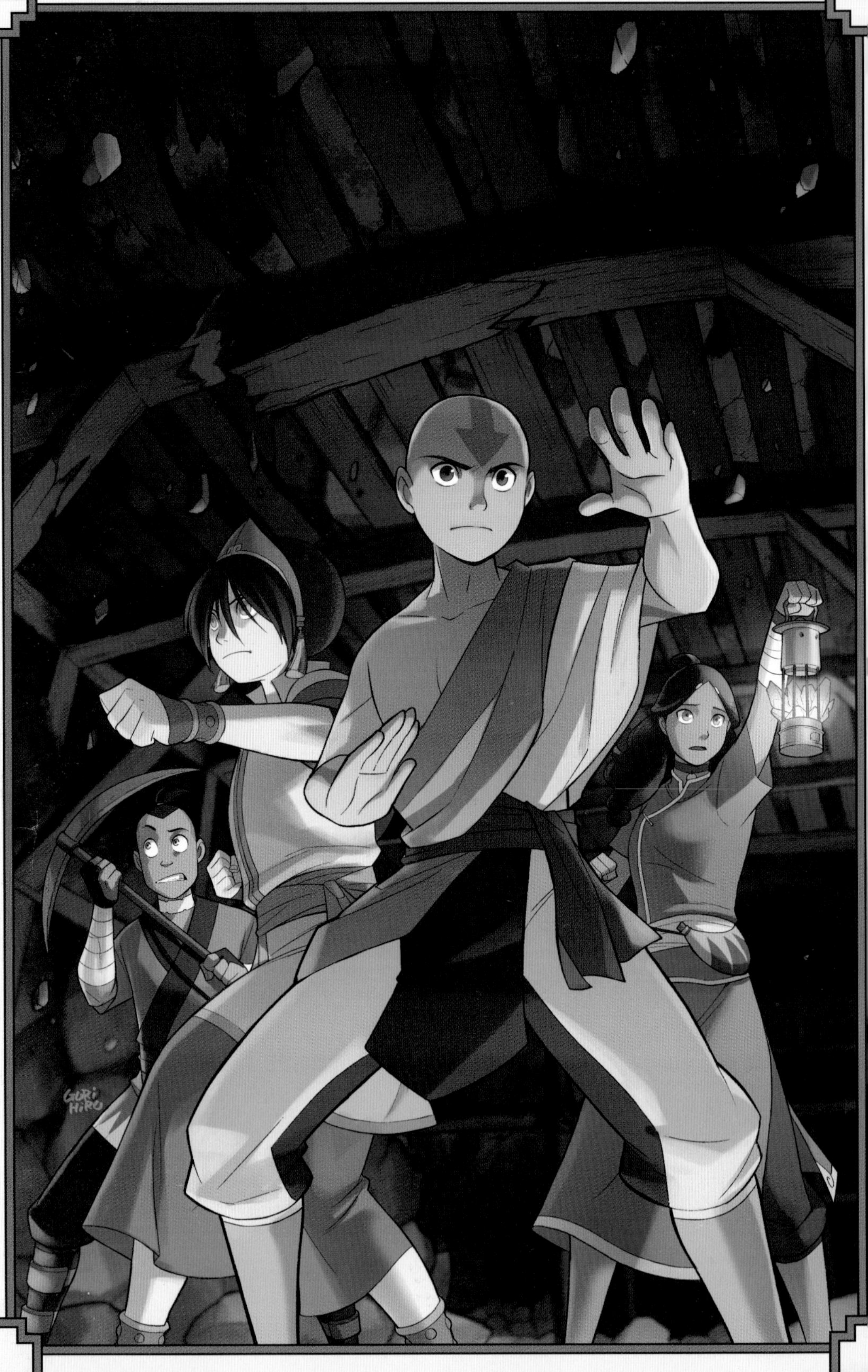
GURI
HIRU

nickelodeon™

降击神通

AVATAR

THE LAST AIRBENDER™

THE RIFT · PART TWO

script
GENE LUEN YANG

art and cover
GURIHIRU

lettering
MICHAEL HEISLER

DARK HORSE BOOKS

president and publisher
MIKE RICHARDSON

collection designer
JUSTIN COUCH

assistant editors
ROXY POLK and AARON WALKER

editor
DAVE MARSHALL

Special thanks to Linda Lee, Kat van Dam, James Salerno, and Joan Hilty
at Nickelodeon, and to Bryan Konietzko and Michael Dante DiMartino.

Published by **Dark Horse Books**
A division of Dark Horse Comics, Inc.
10956 SE Main Street, Milwaukie, OR 97222

DarkHorse.com
Nick.com

International Licensing: (503) 905-2377
Comic Shop Locator Service: (888) 266-4226

First edition: July 2014 | ISBN 978-1-61655-296-1

1 3 5 7 9 10 8 6 4 2
Printed in China

Library of Congress Cataloging-in-Publication Data

Yang, Gene Luen, author.
Avatar the Last Airbender : the rift part two / script, Gene Luen Yang ; art and cover, Gurihiru ; lettering,
Michael Heisler. -- First edition.
pages cm
Summary: As Avatar Aang and his martial arts friends seek answers to the mysteries surrounding a refinery
on land sacred to the Air Nomads, Toph uncovers a startling truth about her father's involvement with the
refinery, while Aang travels to the spirit world, discovering a secret as surprising as it is dangerous.
ISBN 978-1-61655-296-1
1. Graphic novels. [1. Graphic novels. 2. Adventure and adventurers--Fiction. 3. Martial arts--Fiction. 4.
Heroes--Fiction.] I. Gurihiru, illustrators. II. Avatar, the last airbender (Television program) III. Title.
PZ7.7.Y35Aw 2014
741.5'973--dc23

2014006723

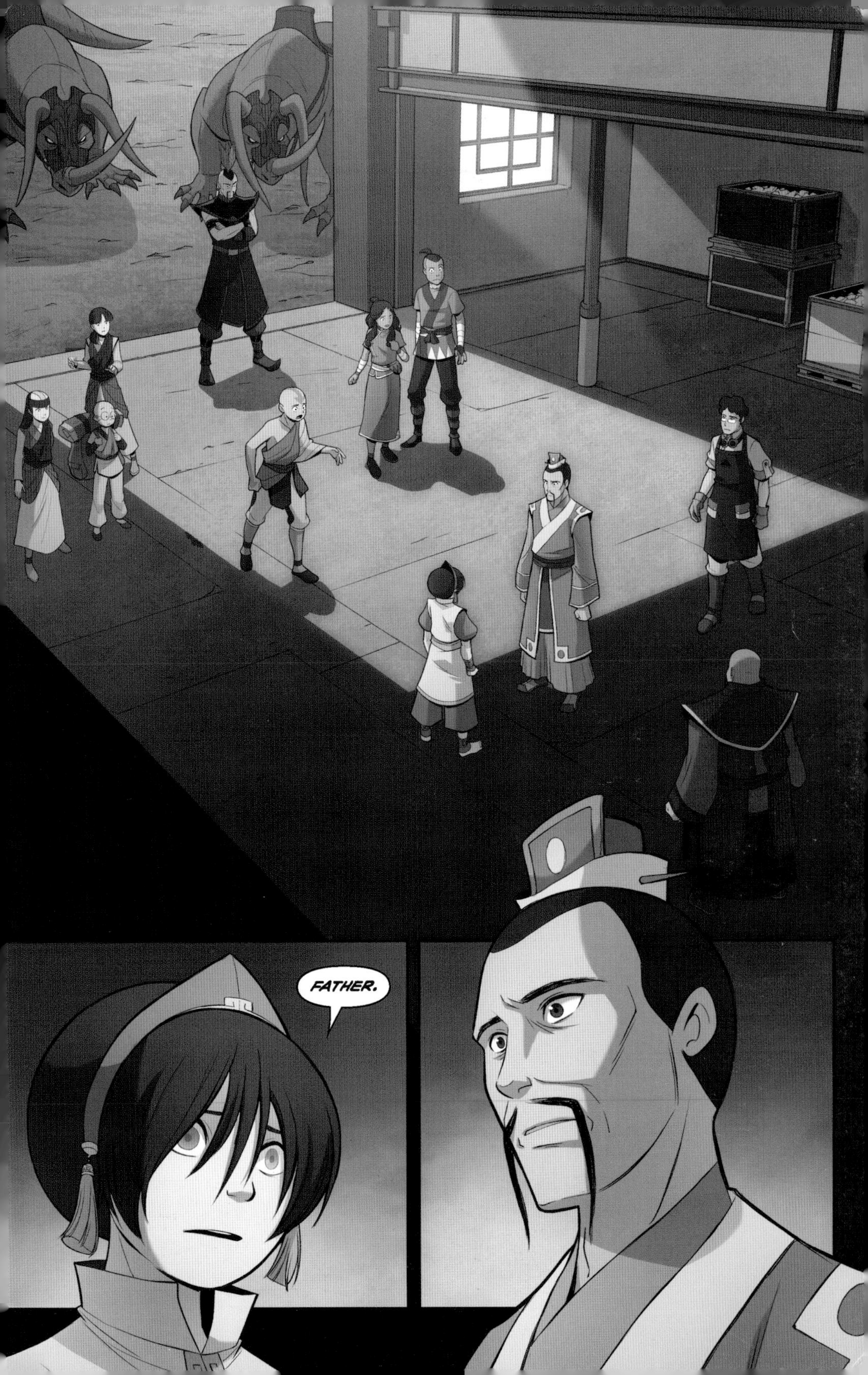
FATHER.

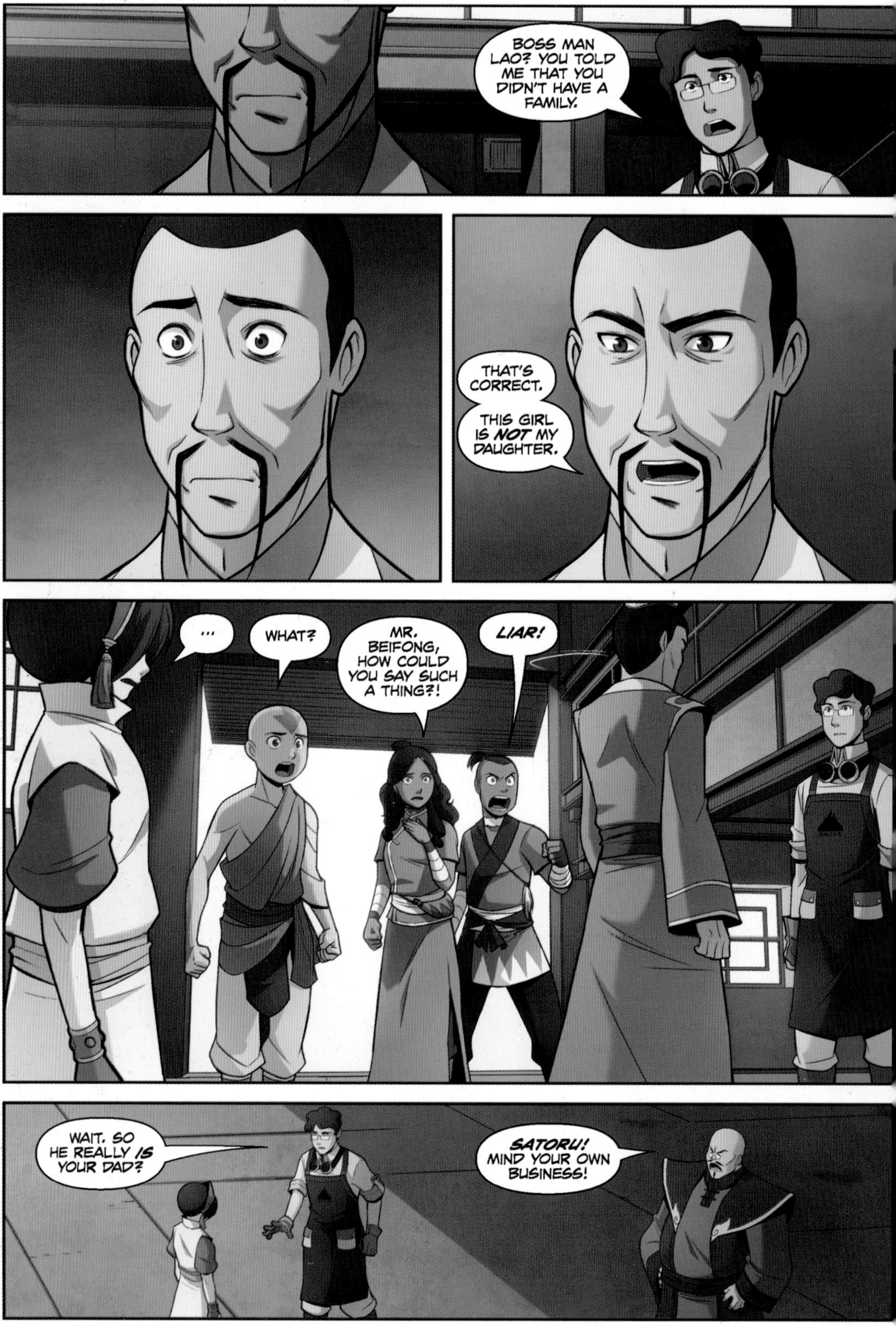
BOSS MAN LAO? YOU TOLD ME THAT YOU DIDN'T HAVE A FAMILY.
THAT'S CORRECT.
THIS GIRL IS *NOT* MY DAUGHTER.
...
WHAT?
MR. BEIFONG, HOW COULD YOU SAY SUCH A THING?!
LIAR!
WAIT. SO HE REALLY *IS* YOUR DAD?
SATORU! MIND YOUR OWN BUSINESS!

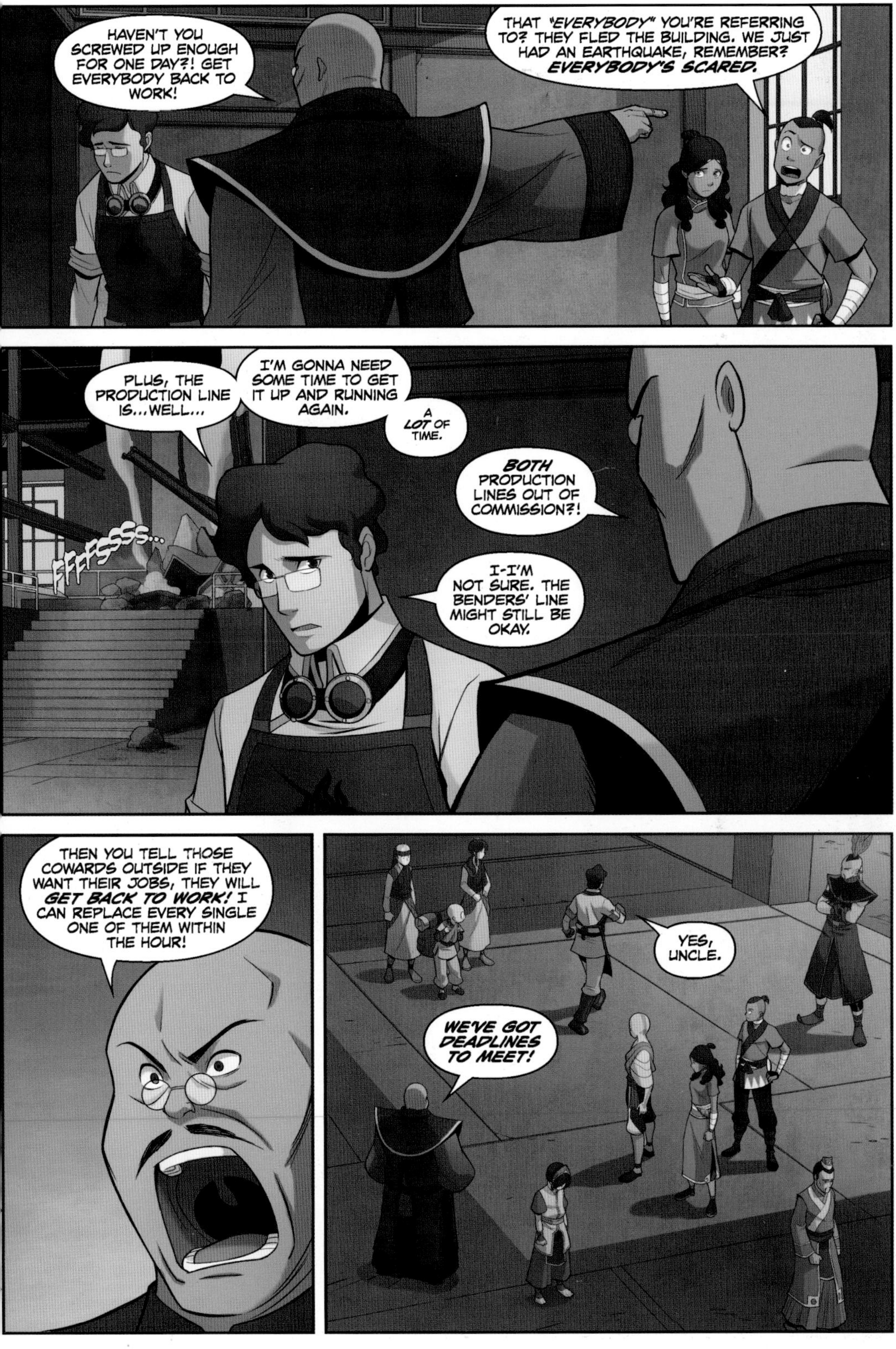
HAVEN'T YOU SCREWED UP ENOUGH FOR ONE DAY?! GET EVERYBODY BACK TO WORK!
THAT "EVERYBODY" YOU'RE REFERRING TO? THEY FLED THE BUILDING. WE JUST HAD AN EARTHQUAKE, REMEMBER? EVERYBODY'S SCARED.
PLUS, THE PRODUCTION LINE IS...WELL...
I'M GONNA NEED SOME TIME TO GET IT UP AND RUNNING AGAIN.
A LOT OF TIME.
FFFFSSSS...
BOTH PRODUCTION LINES OUT OF COMMISSION?!
I-I'M NOT SURE. THE BENDERS' LINE MIGHT STILL BE OKAY.
THEN YOU TELL THOSE COWARDS OUTSIDE IF THEY WANT THEIR JOBS, THEY WILL GET BACK TO WORK! I CAN REPLACE EVERY SINGLE ONE OF THEM WITHIN THE HOUR!
YES, UNCLE.
WE'VE GOT DEADLINES TO MEET!

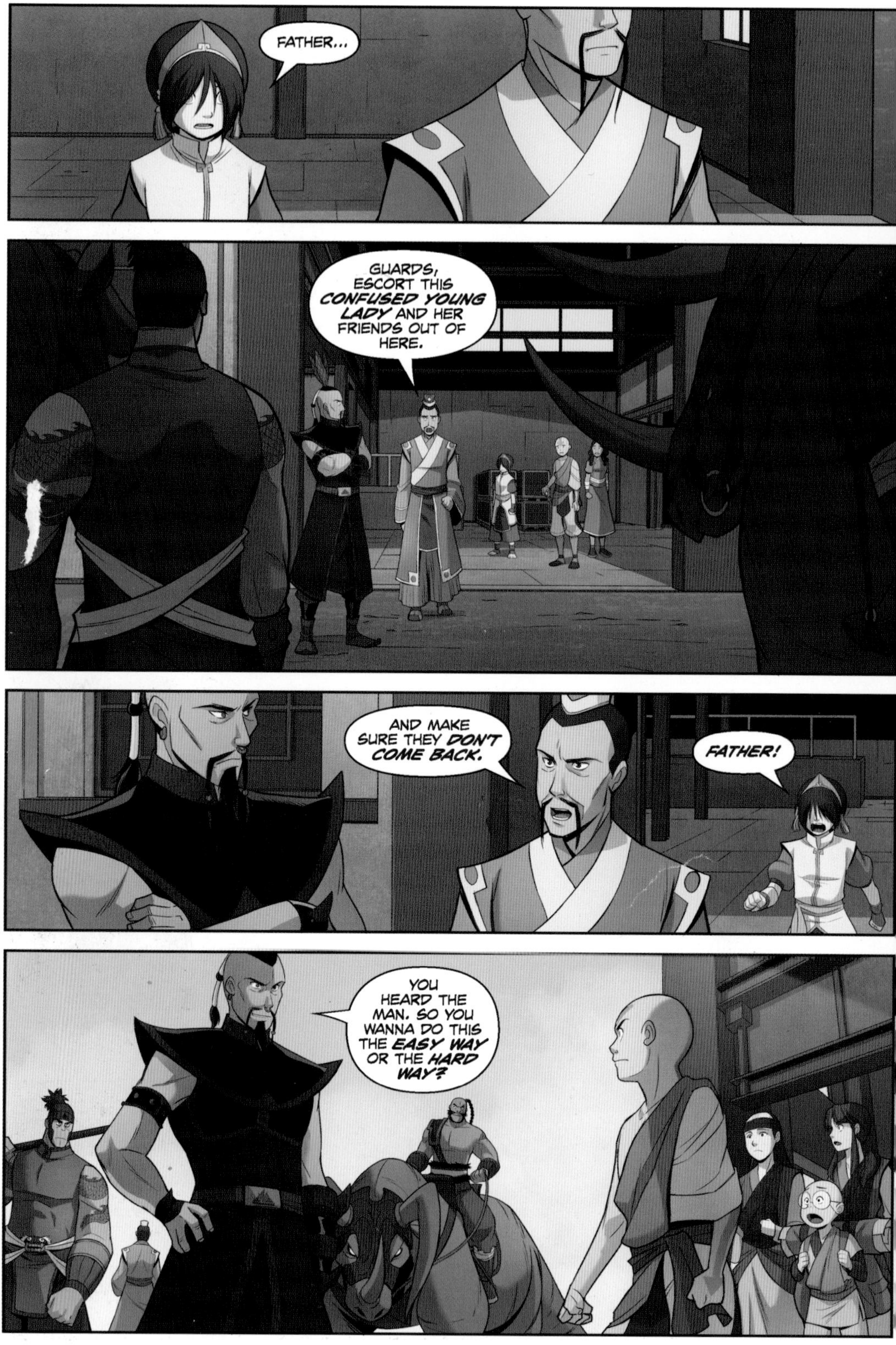
FATHER...
GUARDS, ESCORT THIS CONFUSED YOUNG LADY AND HER FRIENDS OUT OF HERE.
AND MAKE SURE THEY DON'T COME BACK.
FATHER!
YOU HEARD THE MAN. SO YOU WANNA DO THIS THE EASY WAY OR THE HARD WAY?

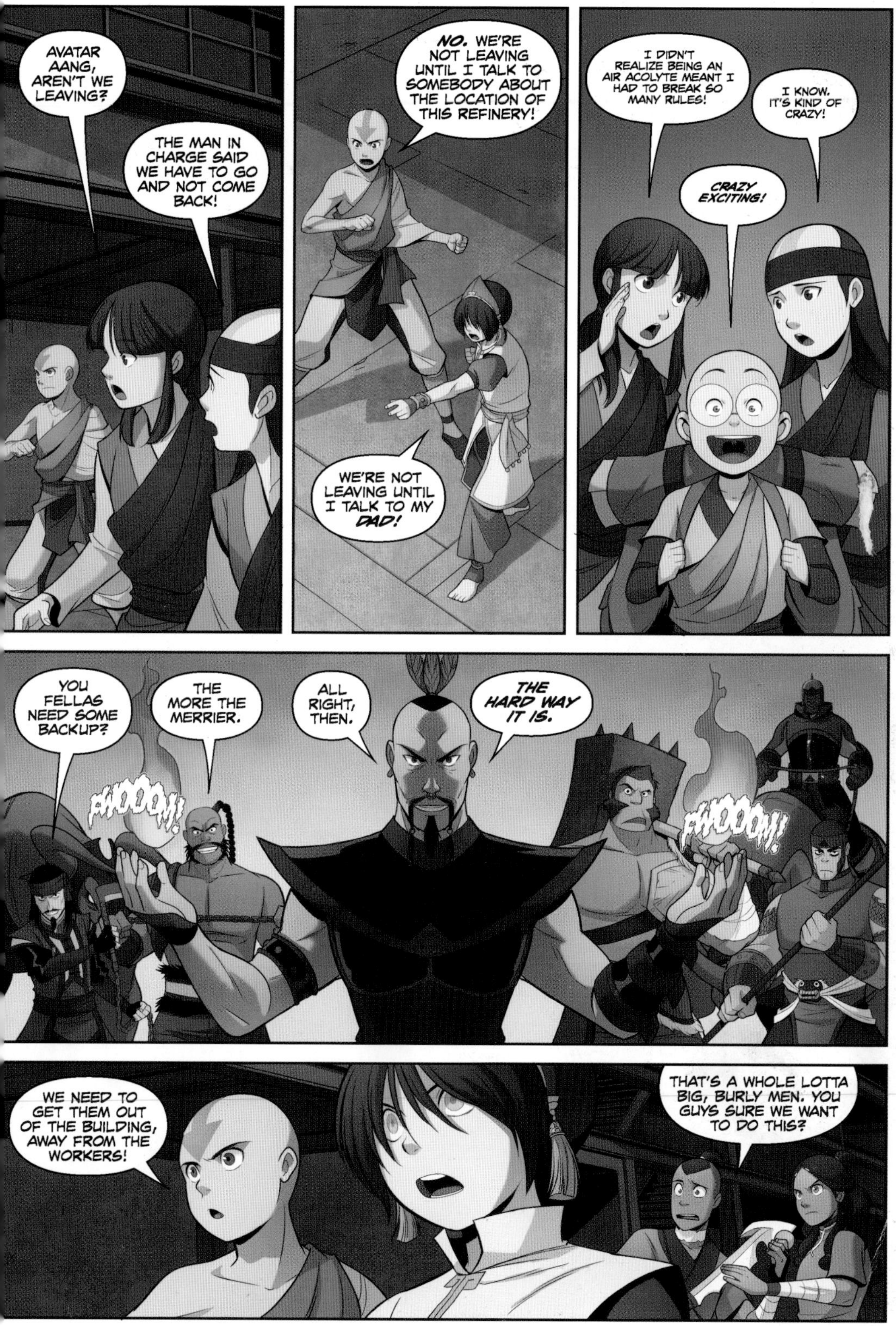
AVATAR AANG, AREN'T WE LEAVING?
THE MAN IN CHARGE SAID WE HAVE TO GO AND NOT COME BACK!
NO. WE'RE NOT LEAVING UNTIL I TALK TO SOMEBODY ABOUT THE LOCATION OF THIS REFINERY!
WE'RE NOT LEAVING UNTIL I TALK TO MY DAD!
I DIDN'T REALIZE BEING AN AIR ACOLYTE MEANT I HAD TO BREAK SO MANY RULES!
I KNOW. IT'S KIND OF CRAZY!
CRAZY EXCITING!
YOU FELLAS NEED SOME BACKUP?
THE MORE THE MERRIER.
FWOOOM!
ALL RIGHT, THEN.
THE HARD WAY IT IS.
FWOOOM!
WE NEED TO GET THEM OUT OF THE BUILDING, AWAY FROM THE WORKERS!
THAT'S A WHOLE LOTTA BIG, BURLY MEN. YOU GUYS SURE WE WANT TO DO THIS?

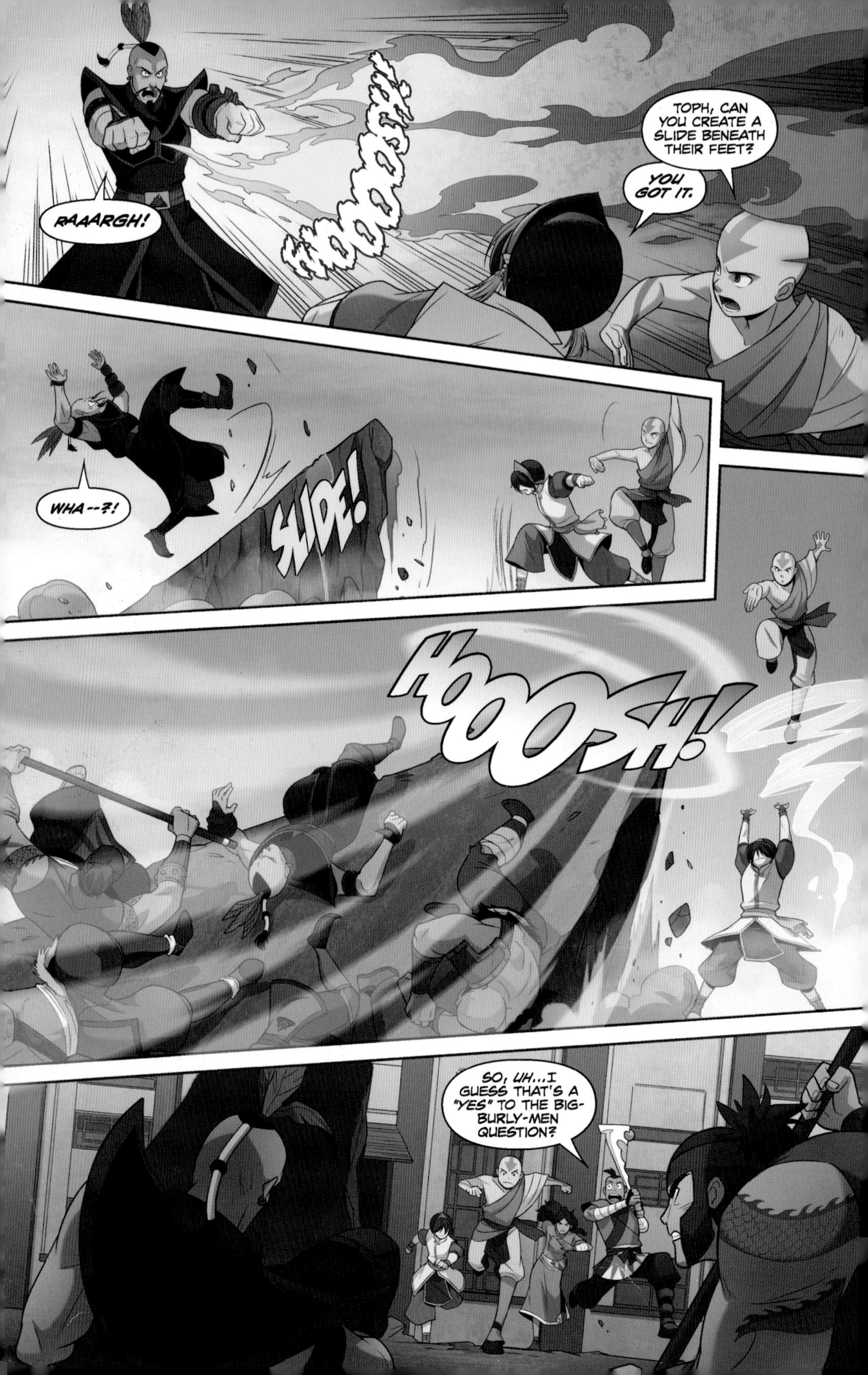
RAAARGH!
FWOOOSH!
TOPH, CAN YOU CREATE A SLIDE BENEATH THEIR FEET?
YOU GOT IT.
WHA--?!
SLIDE!
HOOOOSH!
SO, UH...I GUESS THAT'S A "YES" TO THE BIG-BURLY-MEN QUESTION?

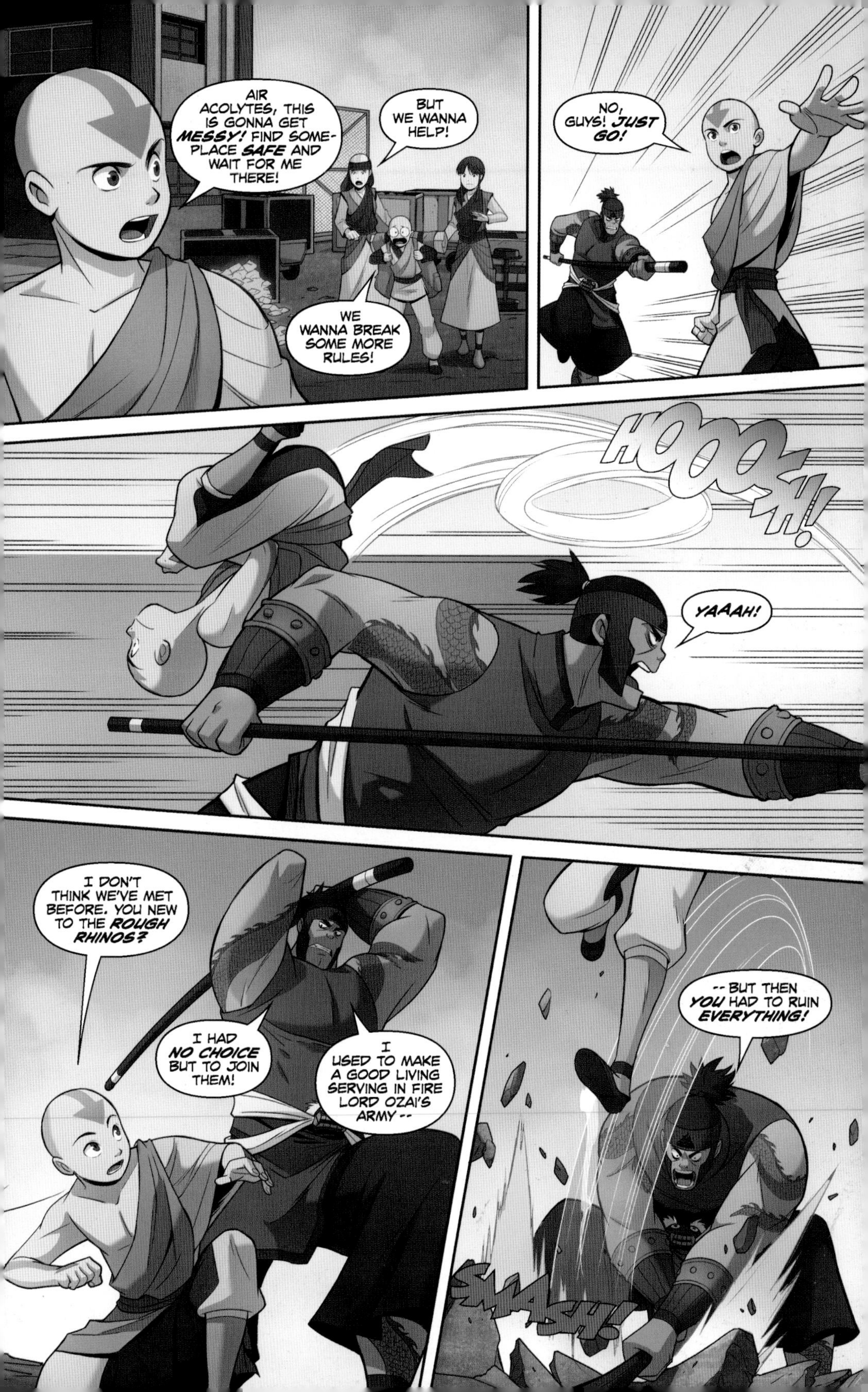
AIR ACOLYTES, THIS IS GONNA GET MESSY! FIND SOME-PLACE SAFE AND WAIT FOR ME THERE!
BUT WE WANNA HELP!
WE WANNA BREAK SOME MORE RULES!
NO, GUYS! JUST GO!
HOOOOH!
YAAAH!
I DON'T THINK WE'VE MET BEFORE. YOU NEW TO THE ROUGH RHINOS?
I HAD NO CHOICE BUT TO JOIN THEM!
I USED TO MAKE A GOOD LIVING SERVING IN FIRE LORD OZAI'S ARMY --
-- BUT THEN YOU HAD TO RUIN EVERYTHING!
SMASH!

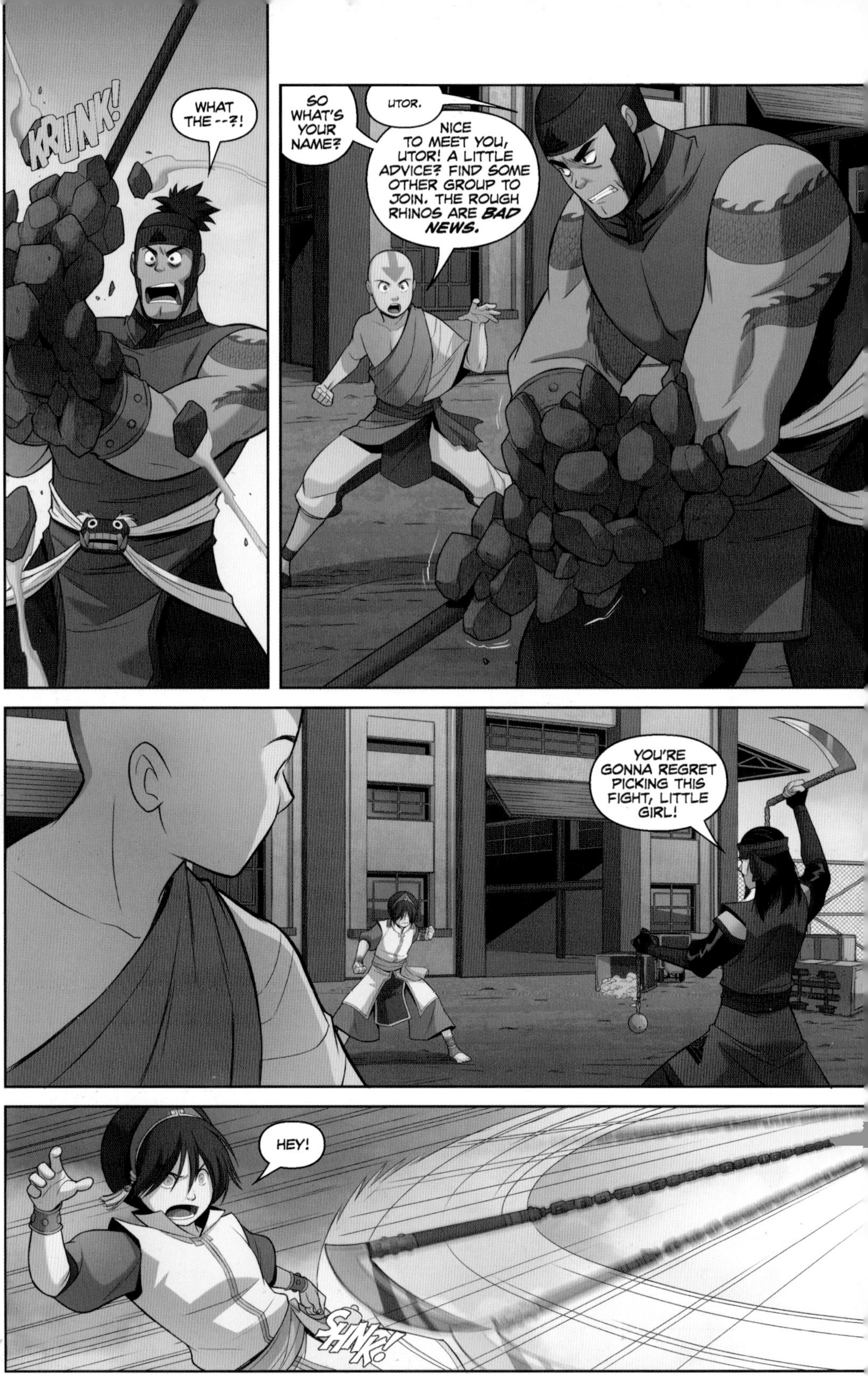
KRUNK!
WHAT THE --?!
SO WHAT'S YOUR NAME?
UTOR.
NICE TO MEET YOU, UTOR! A LITTLE ADVICE? FIND SOME OTHER GROUP TO JOIN. THE ROUGH RHINOS ARE *BAD NEWS.*
YOU'RE GONNA REGRET PICKING THIS FIGHT, LITTLE GIRL!
HEY!
SHINK!

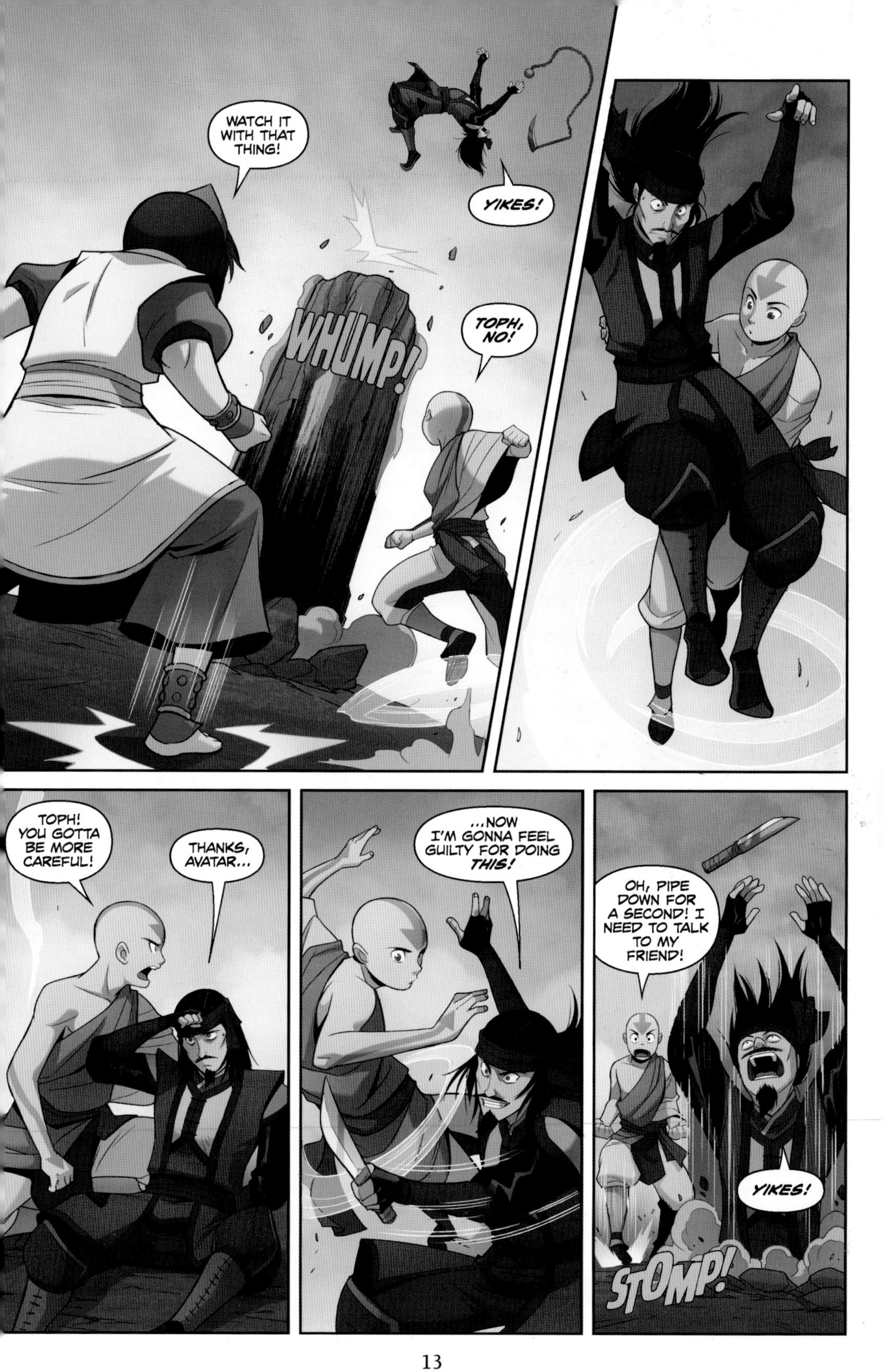
WATCH IT WITH THAT THING!
YIKES!
WHUMP!
TOPH, NO!
TOPH! YOU GOTTA BE MORE CAREFUL!
THANKS, AVATAR...
...NOW I'M GONNA FEEL GUILTY FOR DOING *THIS!*
OH, PIPE DOWN FOR A SECOND! I NEED TO TALK TO MY FRIEND!
YIKES!
STOMP!

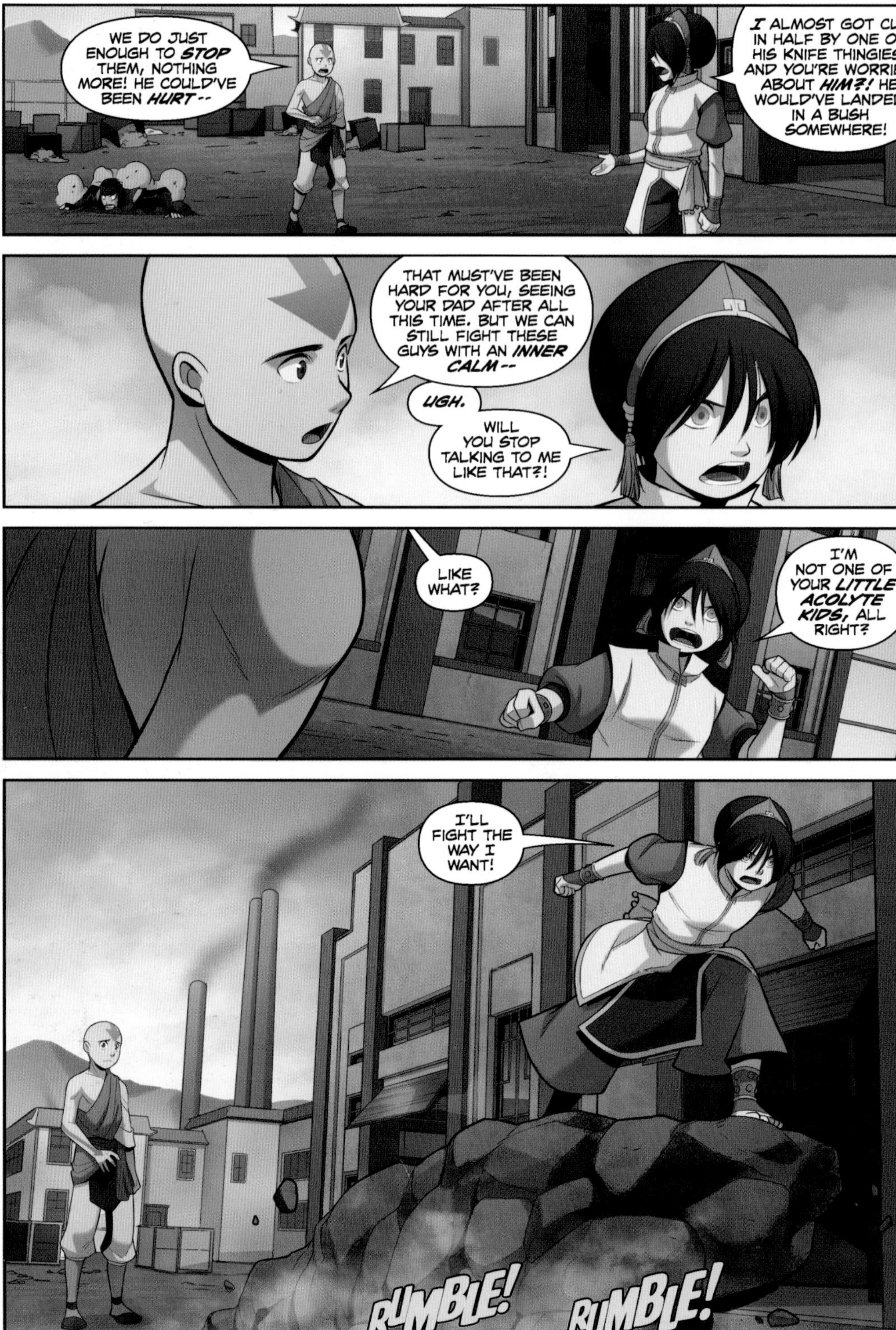
WE DO JUST ENOUGH TO STOP THEM, NOTHING MORE! HE COULD'VE BEEN HURT--
I ALMOST GOT CUT IN HALF BY ONE OF HIS KNIFE THINGIES, AND YOU'RE WORRIED ABOUT HIM?! HE WOULD'VE LANDED IN A BUSH SOMEWHERE!
THAT MUST'VE BEEN HARD FOR YOU, SEEING YOUR DAD AFTER ALL THIS TIME. BUT WE CAN STILL FIGHT THESE GUYS WITH AN INNER CALM--
UGH.
WILL YOU STOP TALKING TO ME LIKE THAT?!
LIKE WHAT?
I'M NOT ONE OF YOUR LITTLE ACOLYTE KIDS, ALL RIGHT?
I'LL FIGHT THE WAY I WANT!
RUMBLE! RUMBLE!

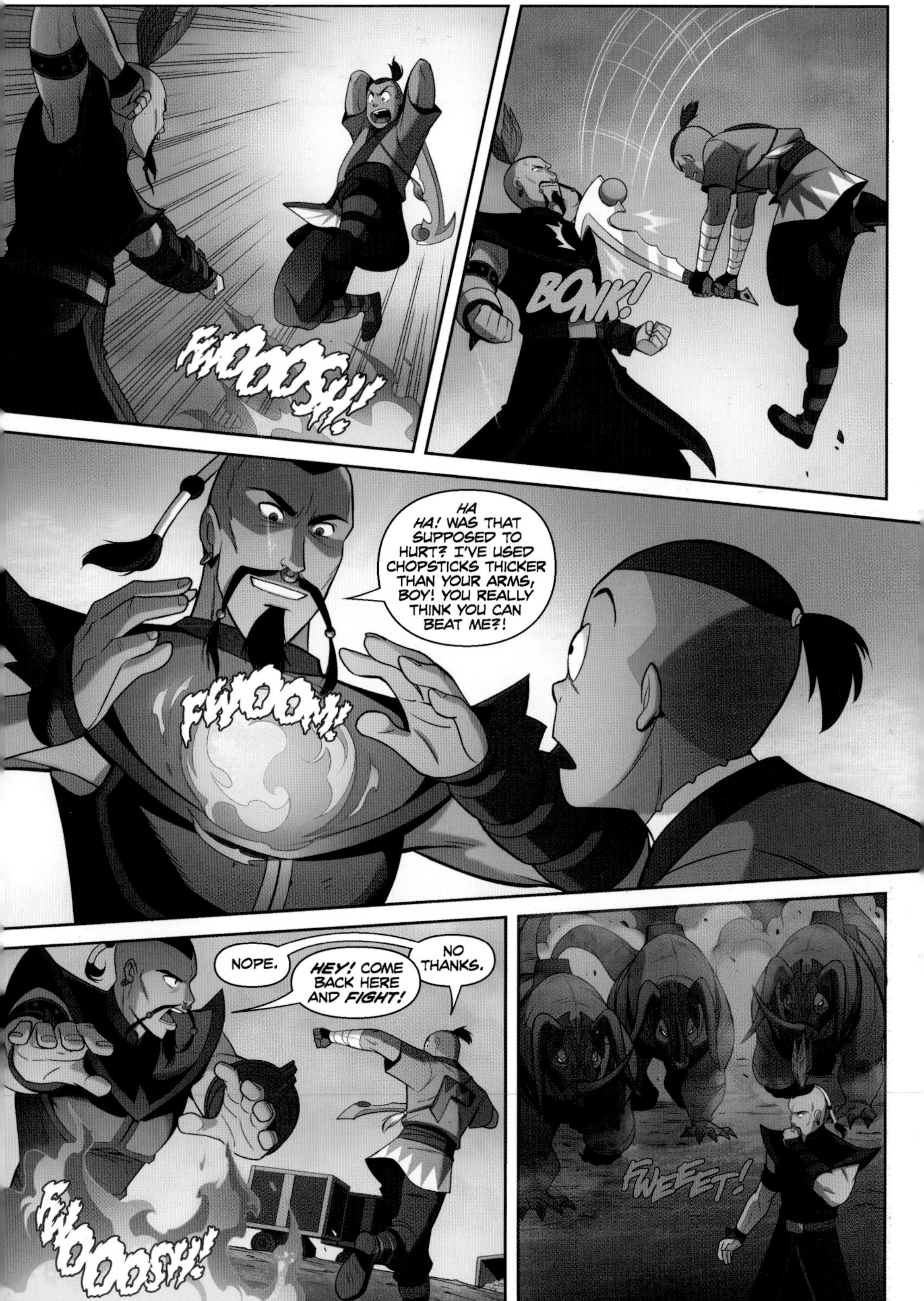
FWOOOSH!
BONK!
HA HA! WAS THAT SUPPOSED TO HURT? I'VE USED CHOPSTICKS THICKER THAN YOUR ARMS, BOY! YOU REALLY THINK YOU CAN BEAT ME?!
FWOOM!
NOPE.
NO THANKS.
HEY! COME BACK HERE AND FIGHT!
FWOOOSH!
FWEEET!

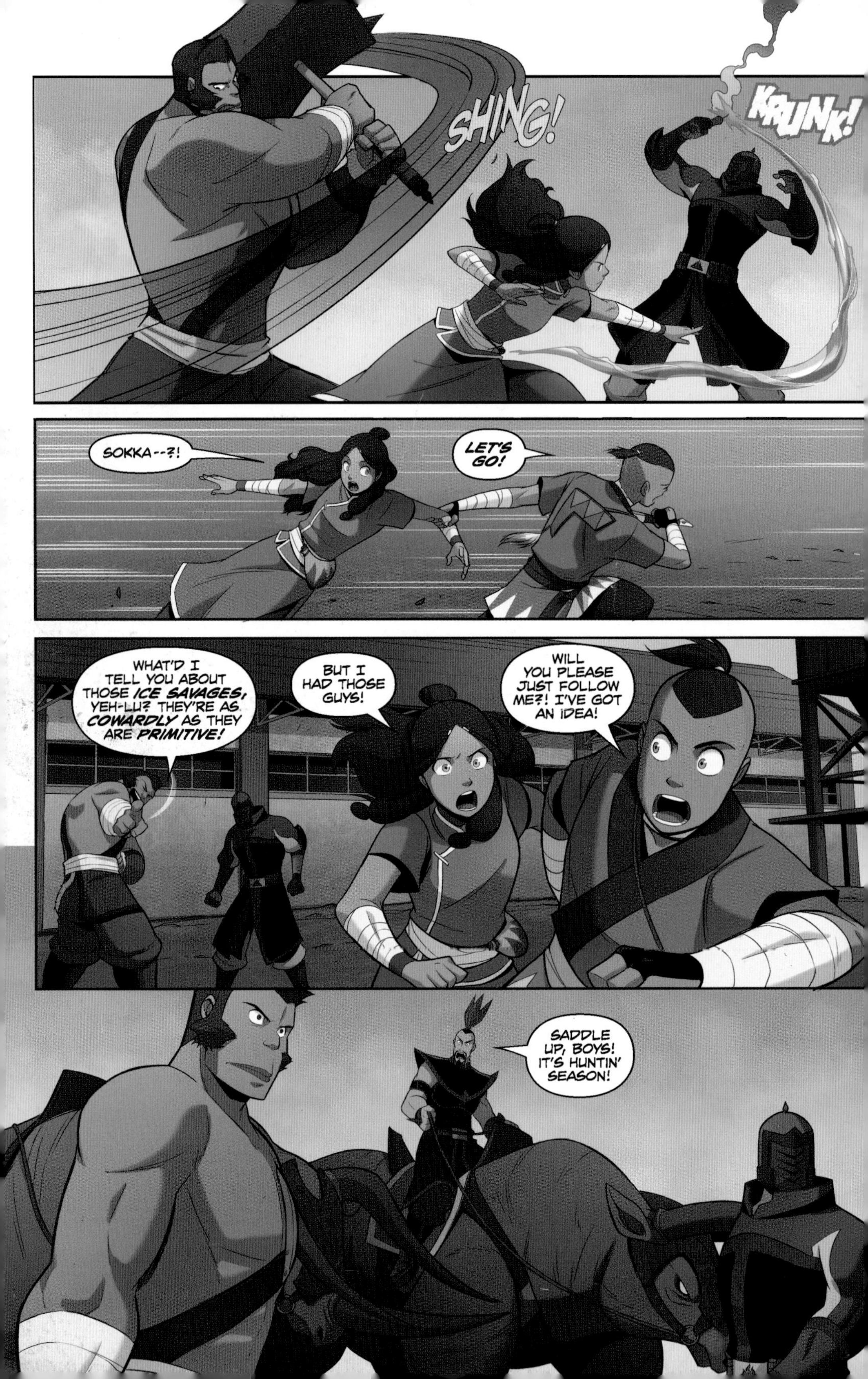
SHING!
KRUNK!
SOKKA--?!
LET'S GO!
WHAT'D I TELL YOU ABOUT THOSE ICE SAVAGES, YEH-LU? THEY'RE AS COWARDLY AS THEY ARE PRIMITIVE!
BUT I HAD THOSE GUYS!
WILL YOU PLEASE JUST FOLLOW ME?! I'VE GOT AN IDEA!
SADDLE UP, BOYS! IT'S HUNTIN' SEASON!

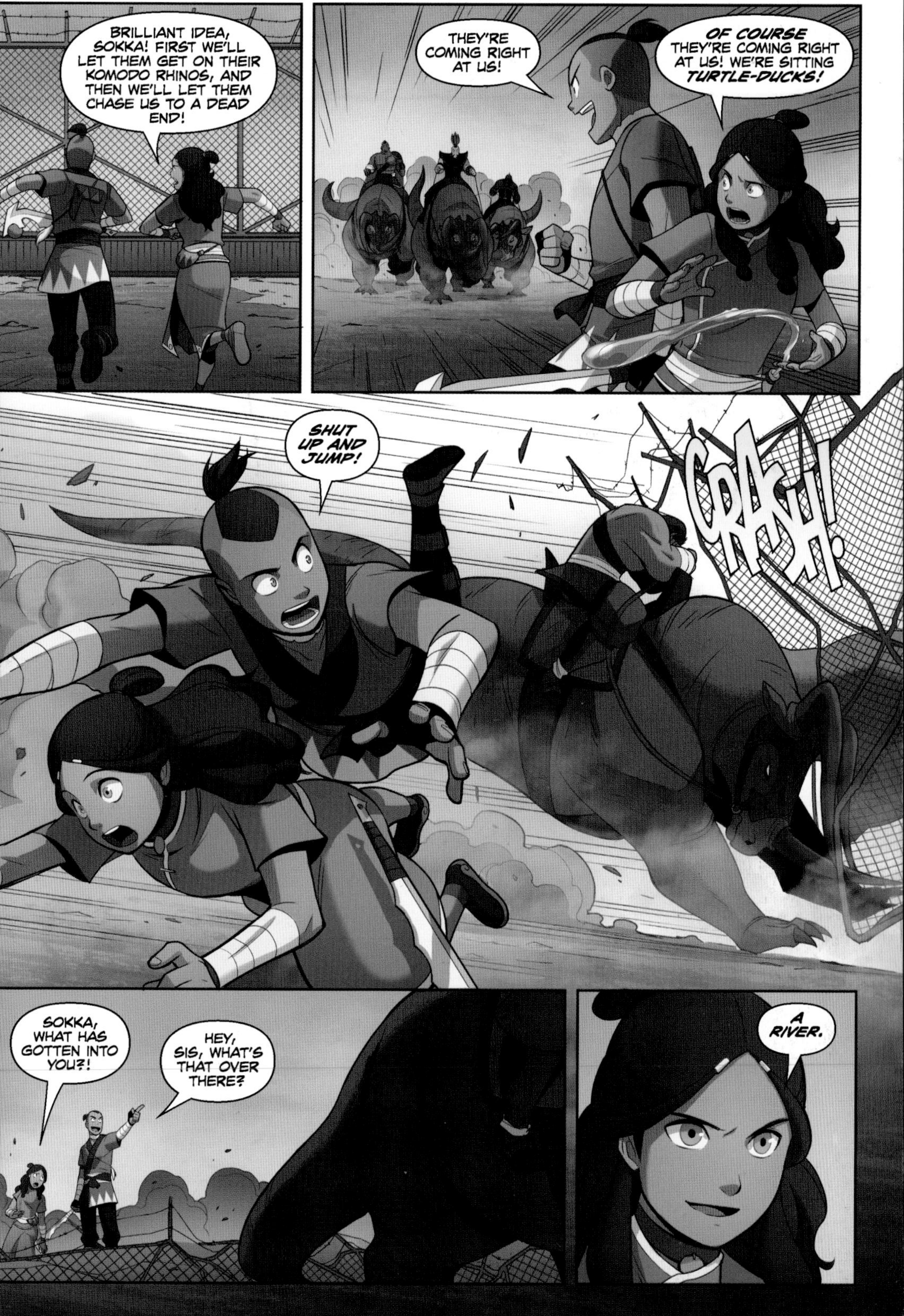
BRILLIANT IDEA, SOKKA! FIRST WE'LL LET THEM GET ON THEIR KOMODO RHINOS, AND THEN WE'LL LET THEM CHASE US TO A DEAD END!
THEY'RE COMING RIGHT AT US!
OF COURSE THEY'RE COMING RIGHT AT US! WE'RE SITTING TURTLE-DUCKS!
SHUT UP AND JUMP!
CRASH!
SOKKA, WHAT HAS GOTTEN INTO YOU?!
HEY, SIS, WHAT'S THAT OVER THERE?
A RIVER.

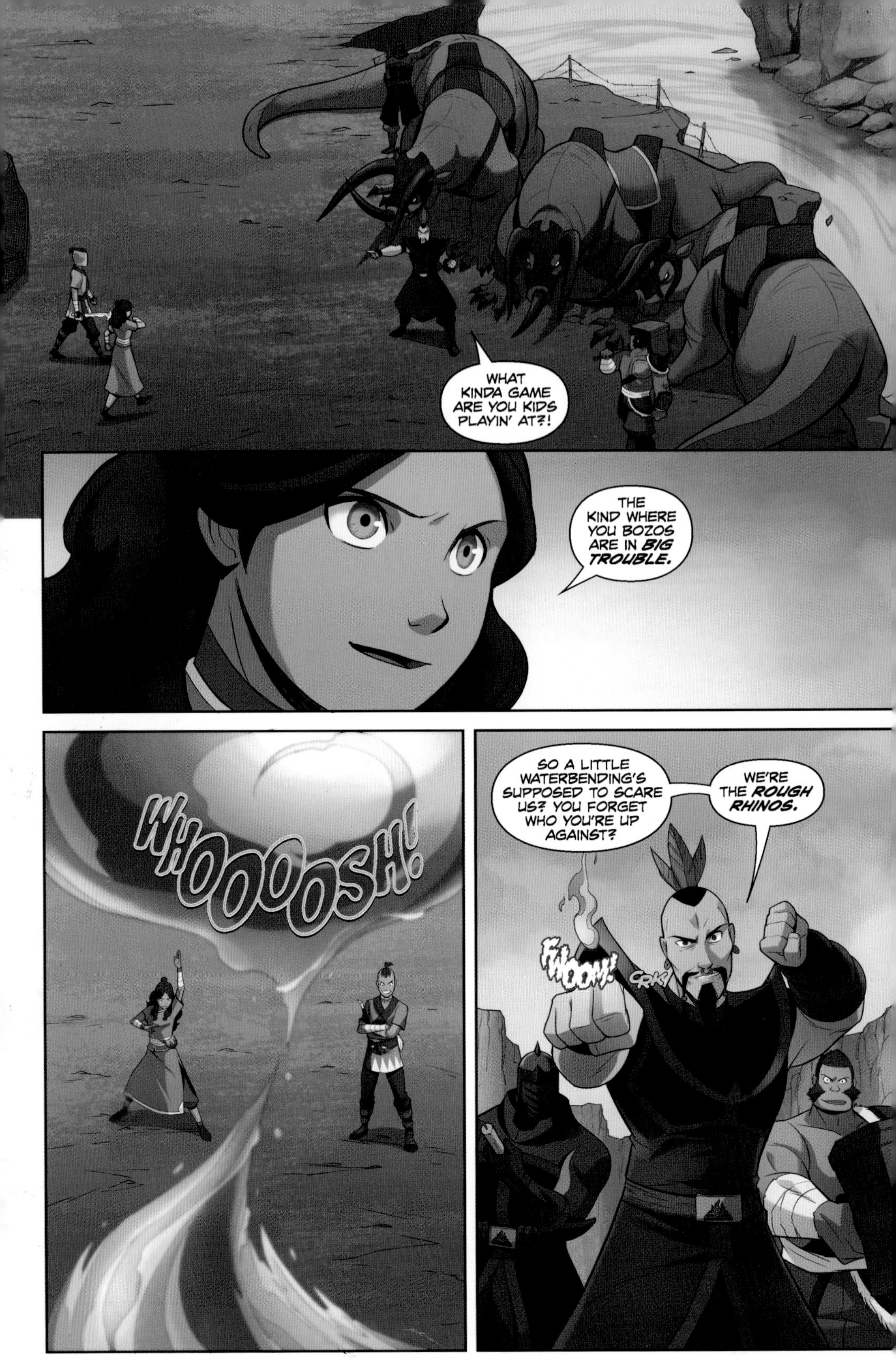
WHAT KINDA GAME ARE YOU KIDS PLAYIN' AT?!
THE KIND WHERE YOU BOZOS ARE IN BIG TROUBLE.
WHOOOOOSH!
SO A LITTLE WATERBENDING'S SUPPOSED TO SCARE US? YOU FORGET WHO YOU'RE UP AGAINST?
WE'RE THE ROUGH RHINOS.
FWOOM!
CRK!

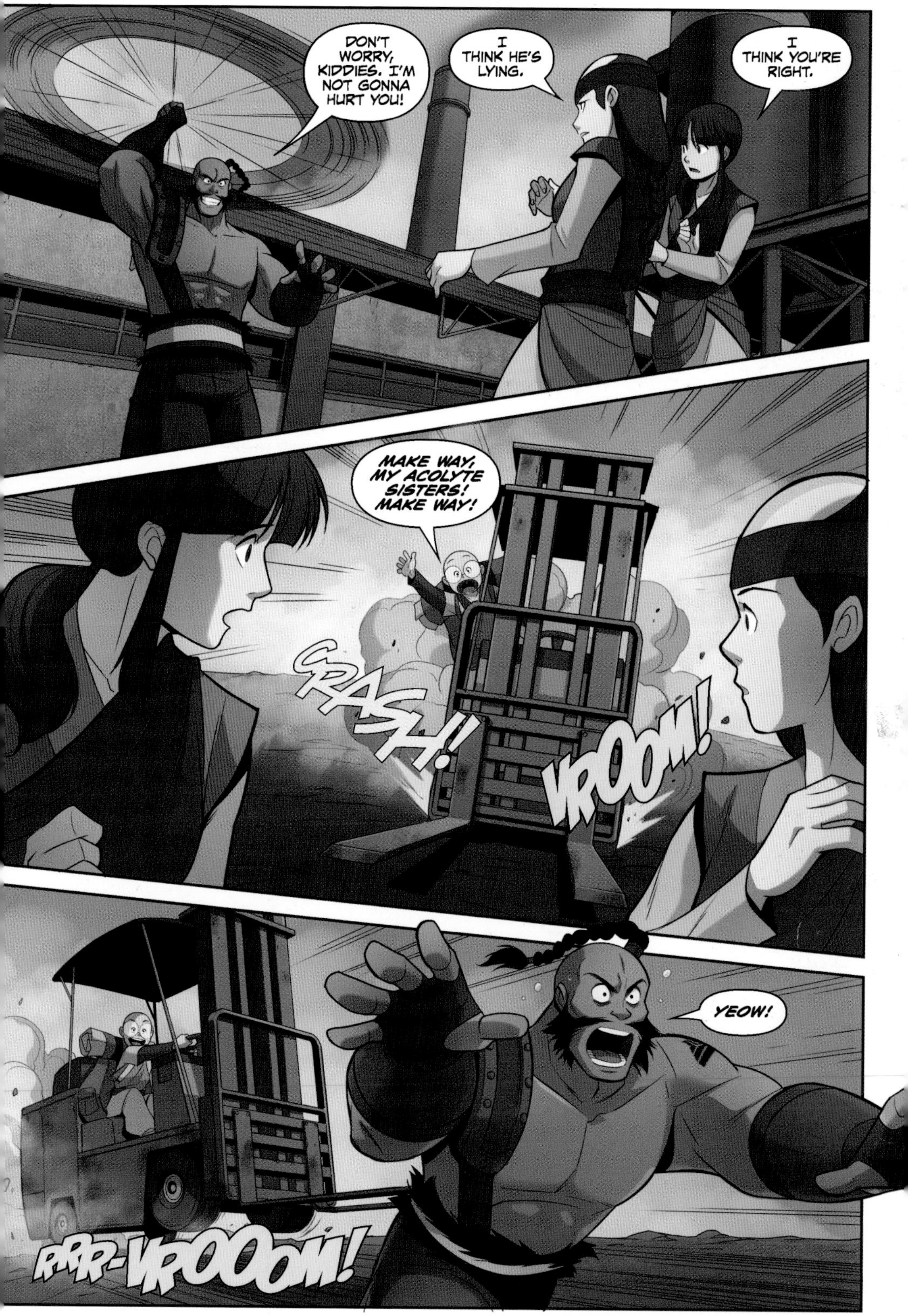
DON'T WORRY, KIDDIES. I'M NOT GONNA HURT YOU!
I THINK HE'S LYING.
I THINK YOU'RE RIGHT.
MAKE WAY, MY ACOLYTE SISTERS! MAKE WAY!
CRASH!
VROOM!
YEOW!
RRR-VROOOM!

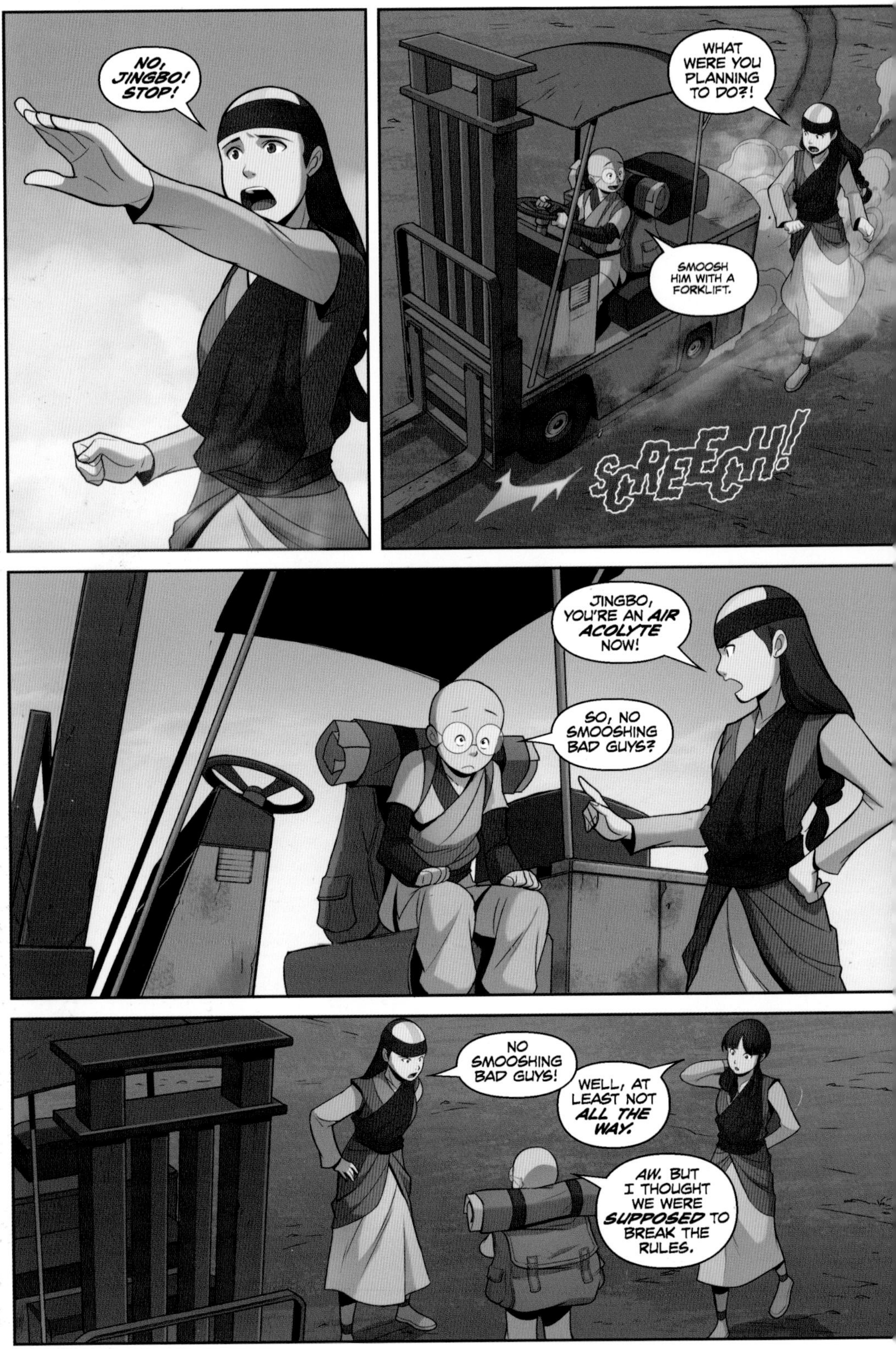

NO, JINGBO! STOP!
WHAT WERE YOU PLANNING TO DO?!
SMOOSH HIM WITH A FORKLIFT.
SCREECH!
JINGBO, YOU'RE AN AIR ACOLYTE NOW!
SO, NO SMOOSHING BAD GUYS?
NO SMOOSHING BAD GUYS!
WELL, AT LEAST NOT ALL THE WAY.
AW. BUT I THOUGHT WE WERE SUPPOSED TO BREAK THE RULES.

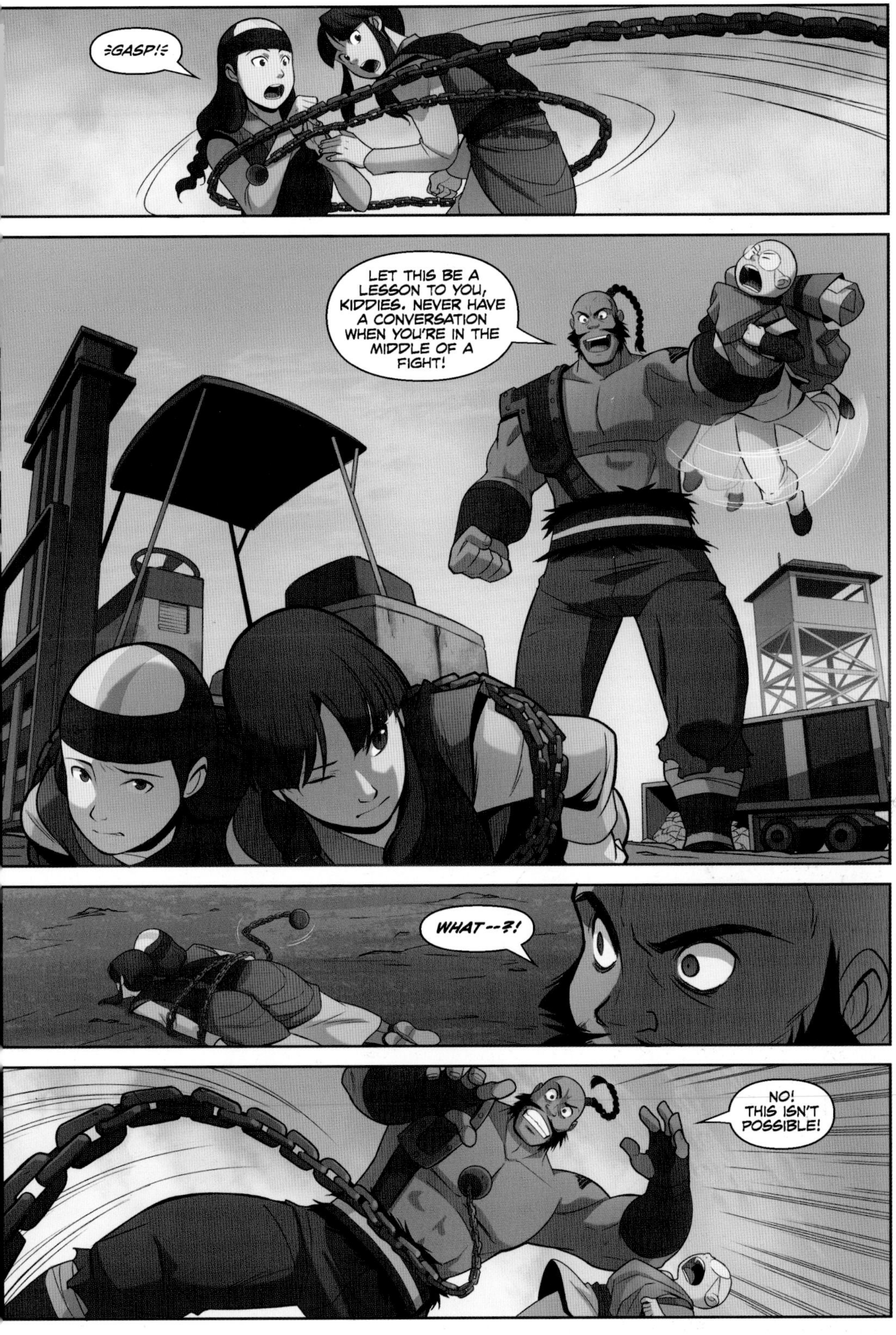

≶GASP!≶
LET THIS BE A LESSON TO YOU, KIDDIES. NEVER HAVE A CONVERSATION WHEN YOU'RE IN THE MIDDLE OF A FIGHT!
WHAT--?!
NO! THIS ISN'T POSSIBLE!

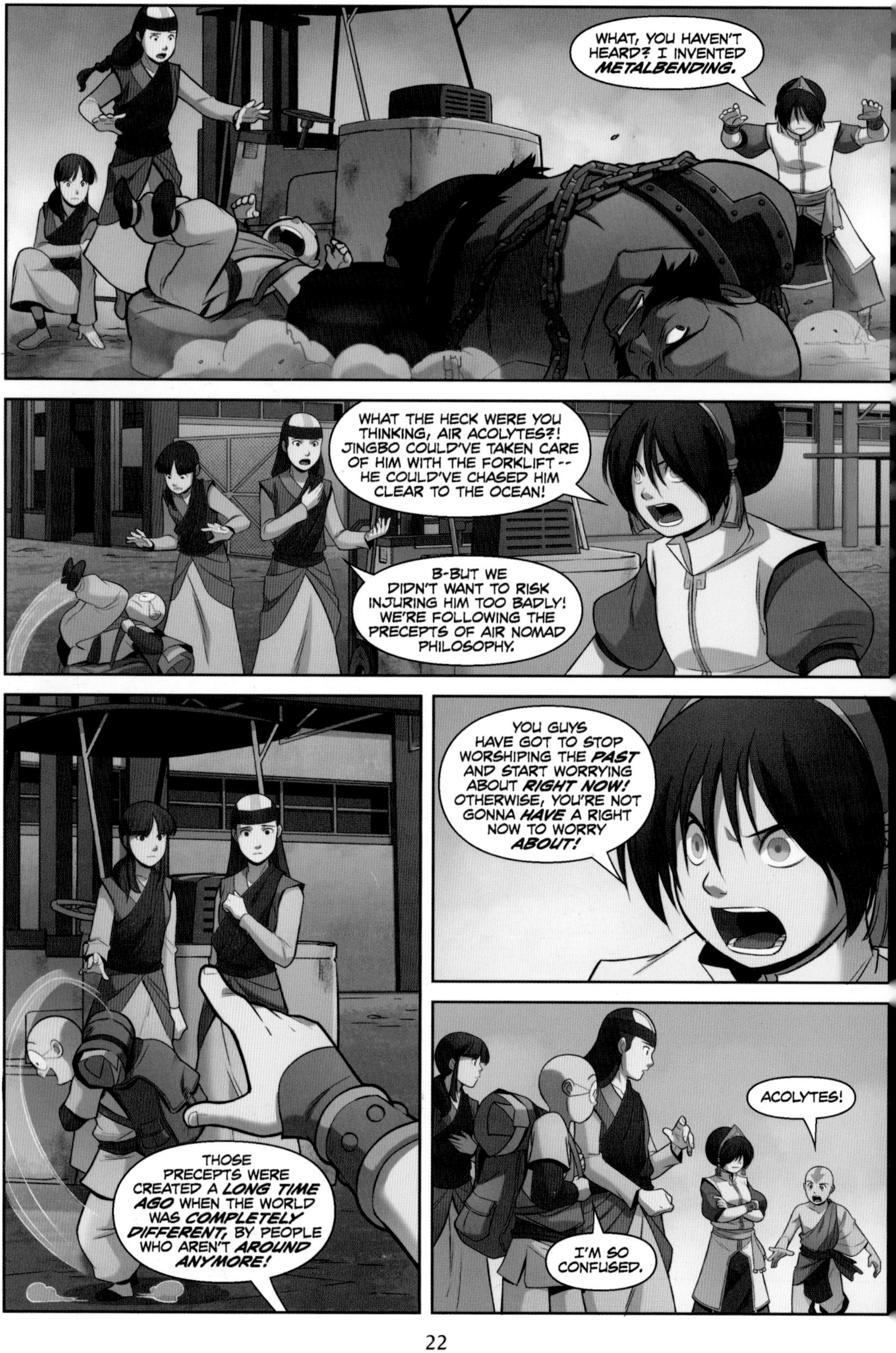
WHAT, YOU HAVEN'T HEARD? I INVENTED METALBENDING.
WHAT THE HECK WERE YOU THINKING, AIR ACOLYTES?! JINGBO COULD'VE TAKEN CARE OF HIM WITH THE FORKLIFT-- HE COULD'VE CHASED HIM CLEAR TO THE OCEAN!
B-BUT WE DIDN'T WANT TO RISK INJURING HIM TOO BADLY! WE'RE FOLLOWING THE PRECEPTS OF AIR NOMAD PHILOSOPHY.
THOSE PRECEPTS WERE CREATED A LONG TIME AGO WHEN THE WORLD WAS COMPLETELY DIFFERENT, BY PEOPLE WHO AREN'T AROUND ANYMORE!
YOU GUYS HAVE GOT TO STOP WORSHIPING THE PAST AND START WORRYING ABOUT RIGHT NOW! OTHERWISE, YOU'RE NOT GONNA HAVE A RIGHT NOW TO WORRY ABOUT!
ACOLYTES!
I'M SO CONFUSED.

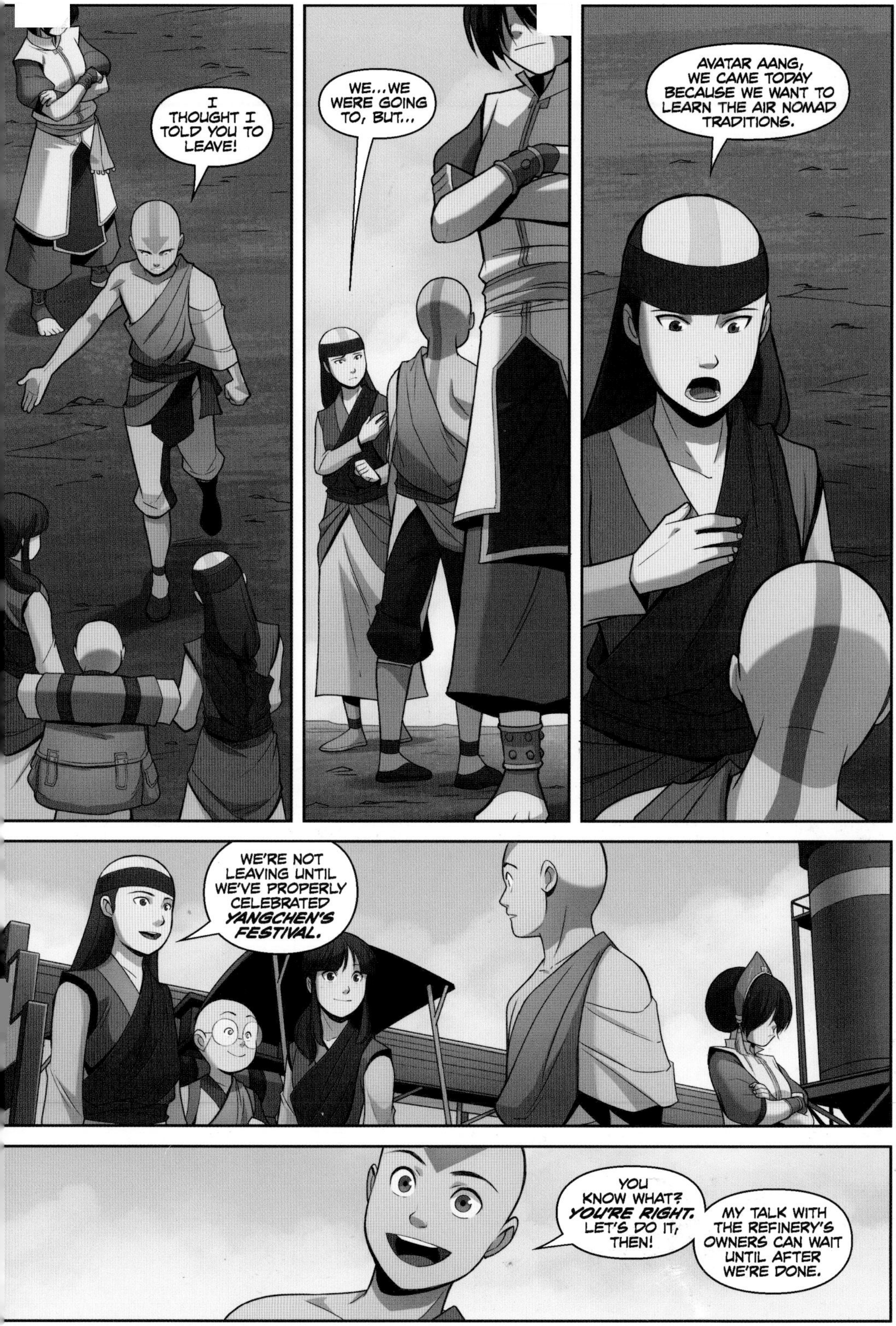

I THOUGHT I TOLD YOU TO LEAVE!
WE...WE WERE GOING TO, BUT...
AVATAR AANG, WE CAME TODAY BECAUSE WE WANT TO LEARN THE AIR NOMAD TRADITIONS.
WE'RE NOT LEAVING UNTIL WE'VE PROPERLY CELEBRATED YANGCHEN'S FESTIVAL.
YOU KNOW WHAT? YOU'RE RIGHT. LET'S DO IT, THEN!
MY TALK WITH THE REFINERY'S OWNERS CAN WAIT UNTIL AFTER WE'RE DONE.

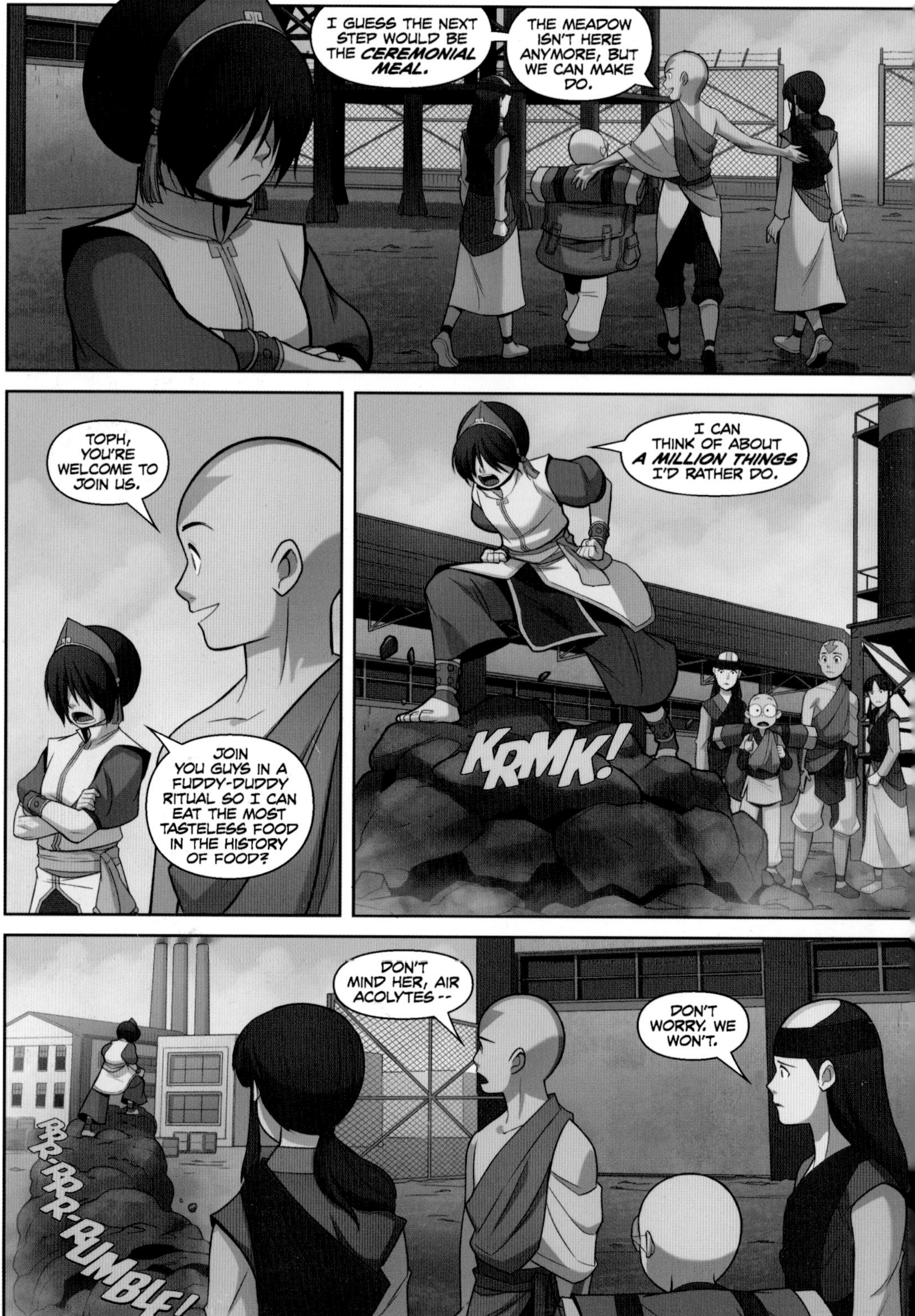
I GUESS THE NEXT STEP WOULD BE THE *CEREMONIAL MEAL.*
THE MEADOW ISN'T HERE ANYMORE, BUT WE CAN MAKE DO.
TOPH, YOU'RE WELCOME TO JOIN US.
JOIN YOU GUYS IN A FUDDY-DUDDY RITUAL SO I CAN EAT THE MOST TASTELESS FOOD IN THE HISTORY OF FOOD?
I CAN THINK OF ABOUT *A MILLION THINGS* I'D RATHER DO.
KRMK!
DON'T MIND HER, AIR ACOLYTES --
DON'T WORRY. WE WON'T.
RR-RR-RR-RUMBLE!

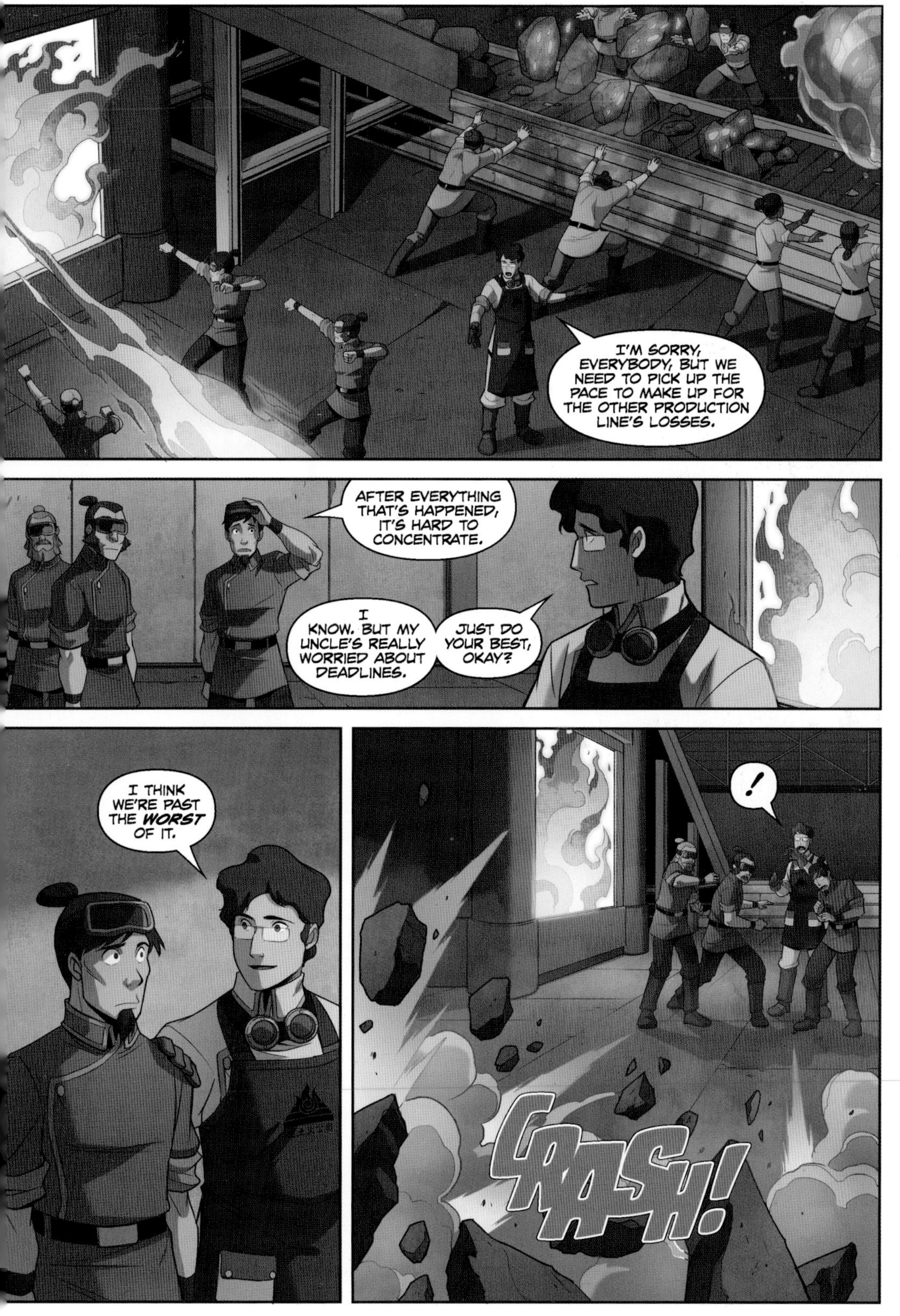
I'M SORRY, EVERYBODY, BUT WE NEED TO PICK UP THE PACE TO MAKE UP FOR THE OTHER PRODUCTION LINE'S LOSSES.
AFTER EVERYTHING THAT'S HAPPENED, IT'S HARD TO CONCENTRATE.
JUST DO YOUR BEST, OKAY?
I KNOW. BUT MY UNCLE'S REALLY WORRIED ABOUT DEADLINES.
I THINK WE'RE PAST THE *WORST* OF IT.
!
CRASH!

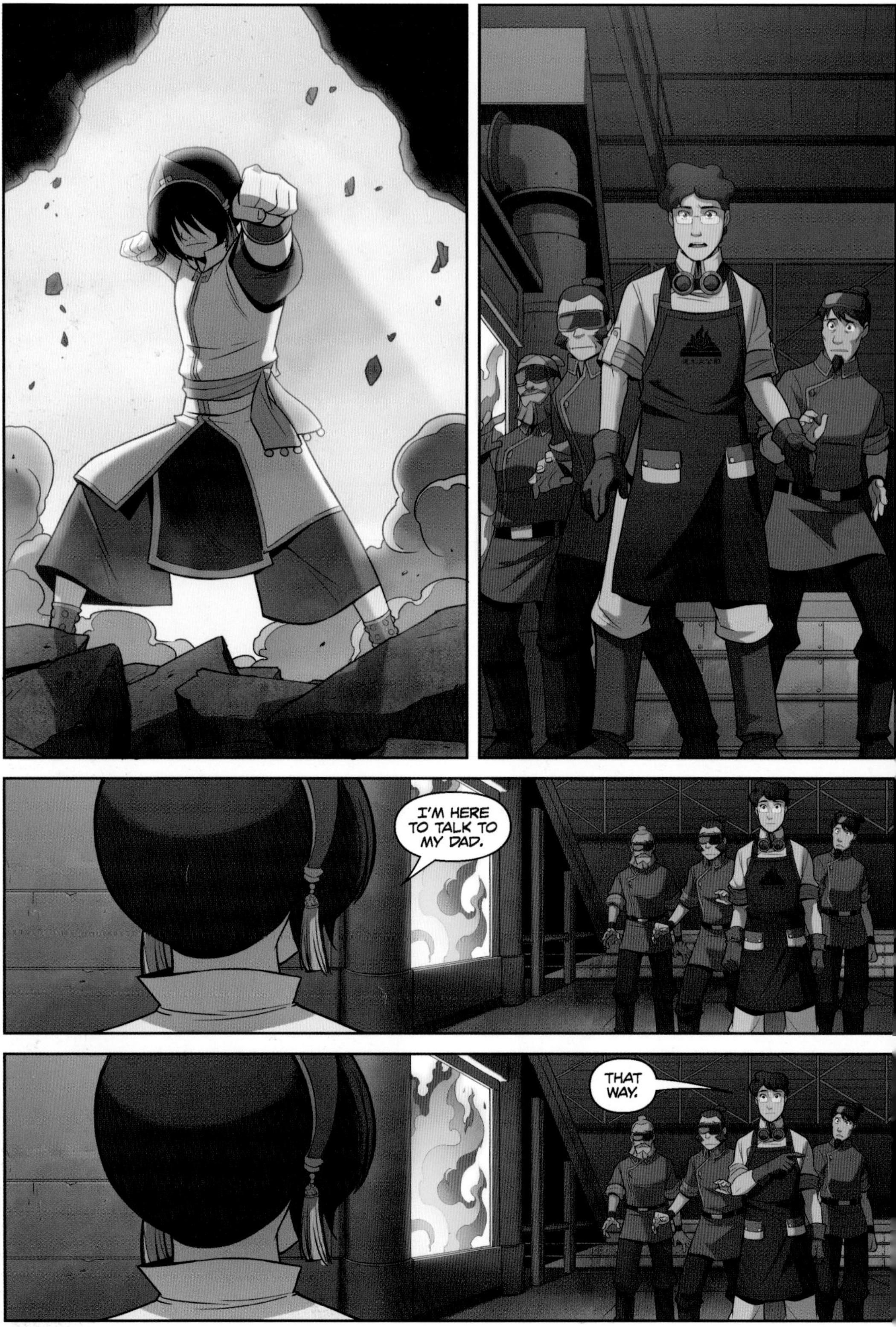
I'M HERE TO TALK TO MY DAD.
THAT WAY.

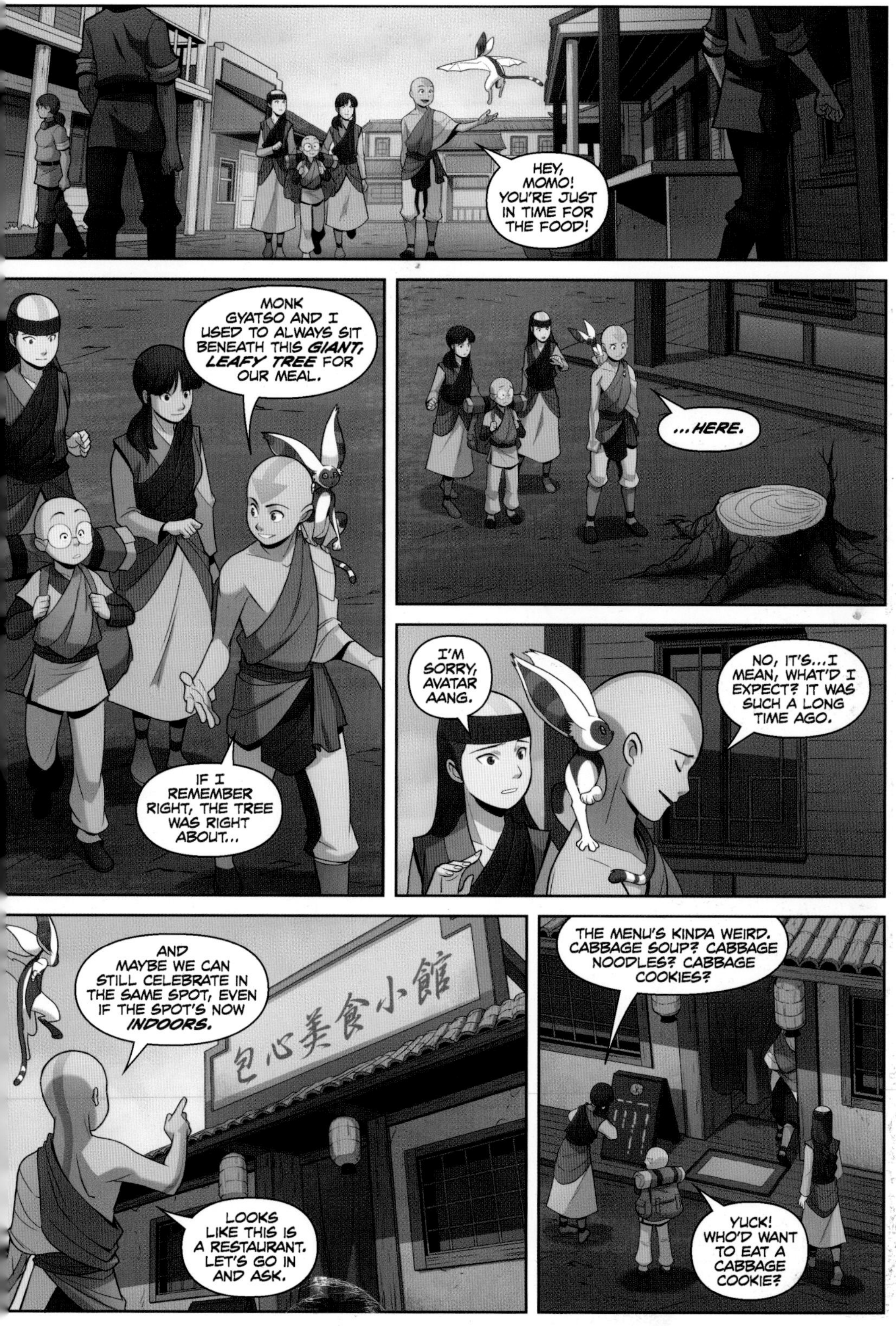
HEY, MOMO! YOU'RE JUST IN TIME FOR THE FOOD!
MONK GYATSO AND I USED TO ALWAYS SIT BENEATH THIS *GIANT, LEAFY TREE* FOR OUR MEAL.
IF I REMEMBER RIGHT, THE TREE WAS RIGHT ABOUT...
...*HERE.*
I'M SORRY, AVATAR AANG.
NO, IT'S...I MEAN, WHAT'D I EXPECT? IT WAS SUCH A LONG TIME AGO.
AND MAYBE WE CAN STILL CELEBRATE IN THE SAME SPOT, EVEN IF THE SPOT'S NOW *INDOORS.*
包心美食小館
LOOKS LIKE THIS IS A RESTAURANT. LET'S GO IN AND ASK.
THE MENU'S KINDA WEIRD. CABBAGE SOUP? CABBAGE NOODLES? CABBAGE COOKIES?
YUCK! WHO'D WANT TO EAT A CABBAGE COOKIE?

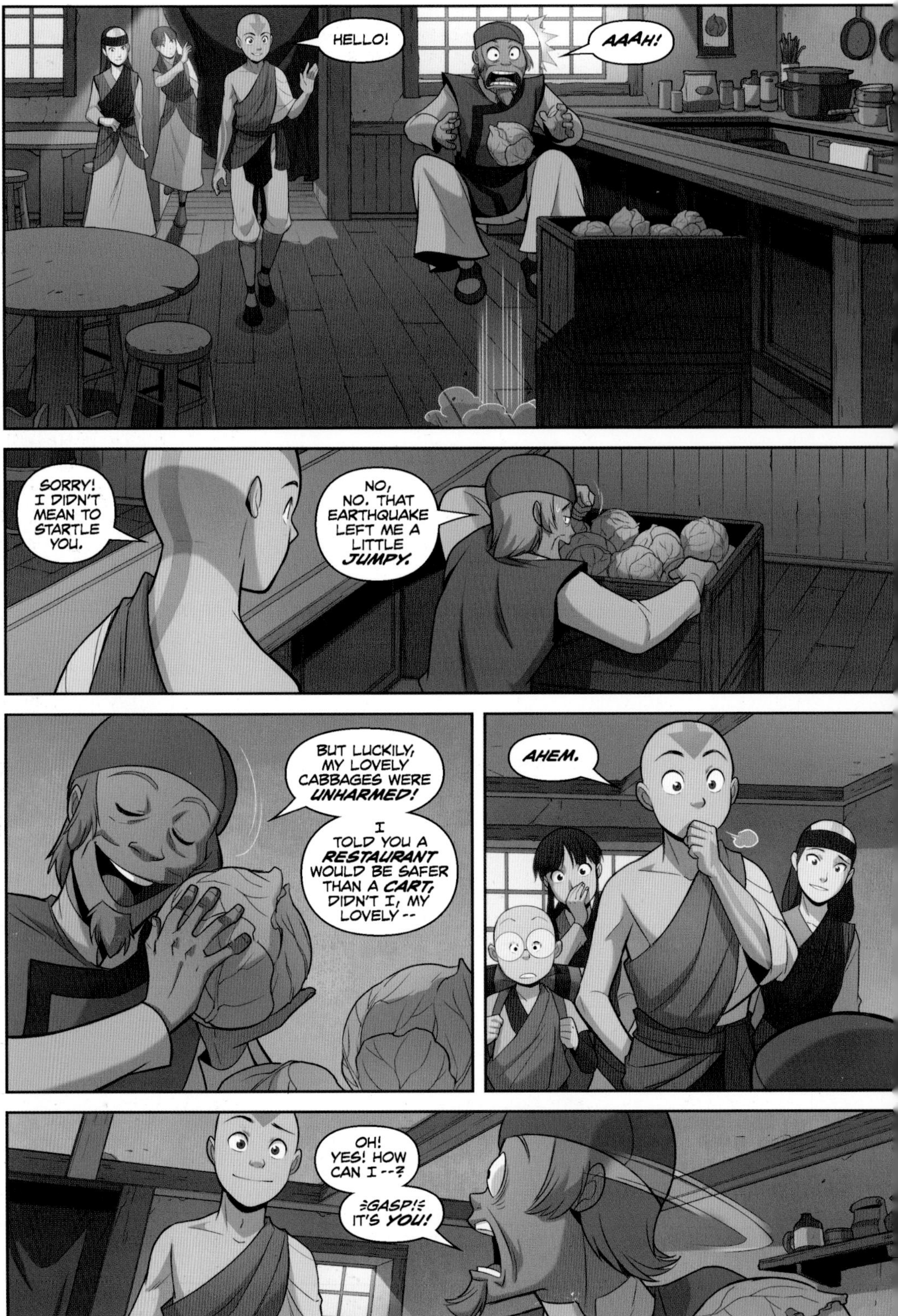
HELLO!
AAAH!
SORRY! I DIDN'T MEAN TO STARTLE YOU.
NO, NO. THAT EARTHQUAKE LEFT ME A LITTLE JUMPY.
BUT LUCKILY, MY LOVELY CABBAGES WERE UNHARMED!
I TOLD YOU A RESTAURANT WOULD BE SAFER THAN A CART, DIDN'T I, MY LOVELY --
AHEM.
OH! YES! HOW CAN I --?
GASP! IT'S YOU!

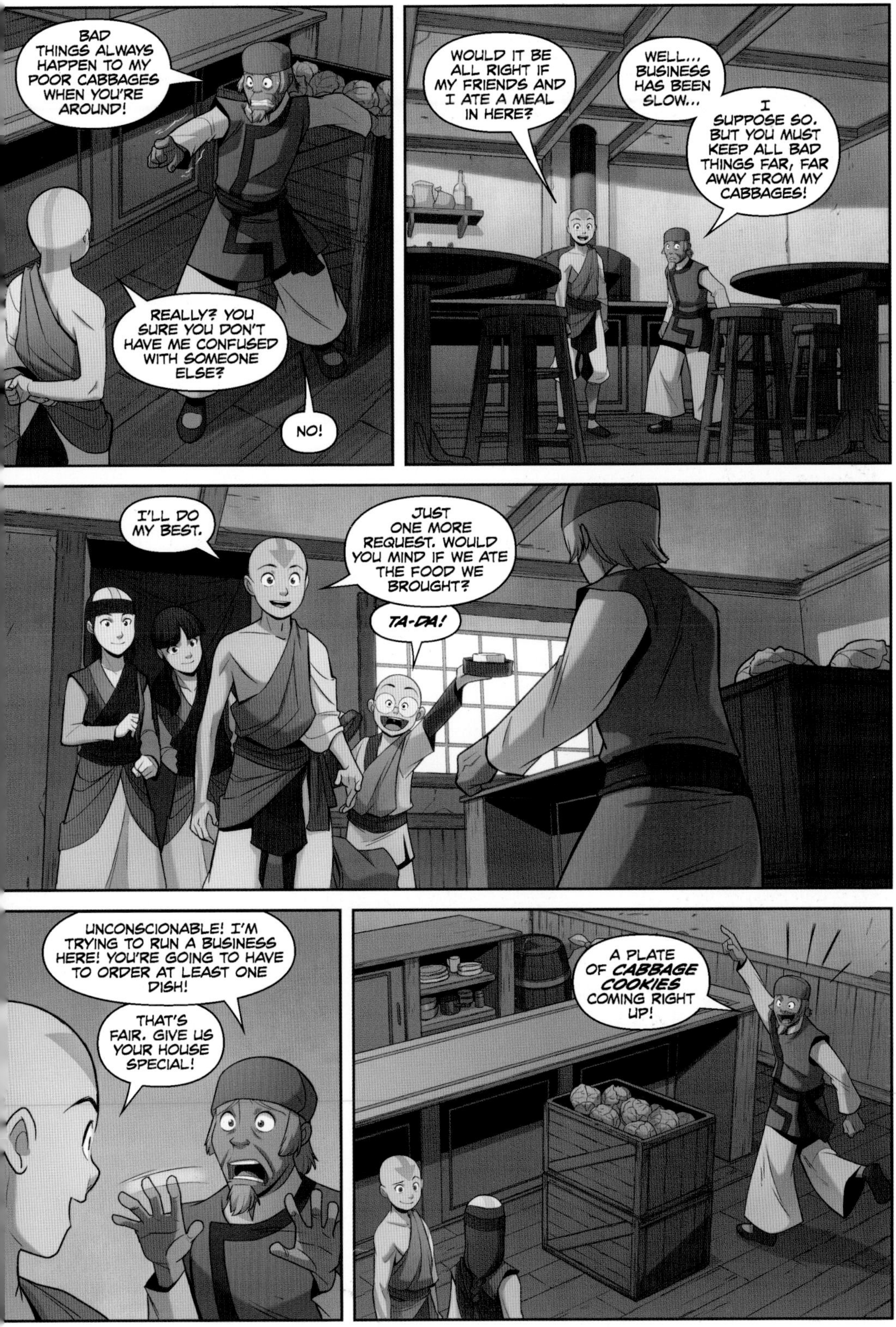
BAD THINGS ALWAYS HAPPEN TO MY POOR CABBAGES WHEN YOU'RE AROUND!
REALLY? YOU SURE YOU DON'T HAVE ME CONFUSED WITH SOMEONE ELSE?
NO!
WOULD IT BE ALL RIGHT IF MY FRIENDS AND I ATE A MEAL IN HERE?
WELL... BUSINESS HAS BEEN SLOW...
I SUPPOSE SO. BUT YOU MUST KEEP ALL BAD THINGS FAR, FAR AWAY FROM MY CABBAGES!
I'LL DO MY BEST.
JUST ONE MORE REQUEST. WOULD YOU MIND IF WE ATE THE FOOD WE BROUGHT?
TA-DA!
UNCONSCIONABLE! I'M TRYING TO RUN A BUSINESS HERE! YOU'RE GOING TO HAVE TO ORDER AT LEAST ONE DISH!
THAT'S FAIR. GIVE US YOUR HOUSE SPECIAL!
A PLATE OF CABBAGE COOKIES COMING RIGHT UP!

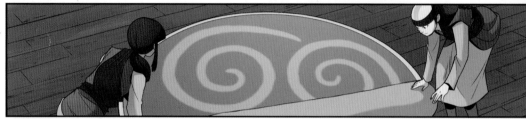

HERE YOU GO, FRESH FROM THE OVEN! ENJOY!

HM. NOT BAD. TASTES KINDA LIKE A SUGAR COOKIE--

--ONLY MORE *CABBAGEY.*

SNIFF SNIFF

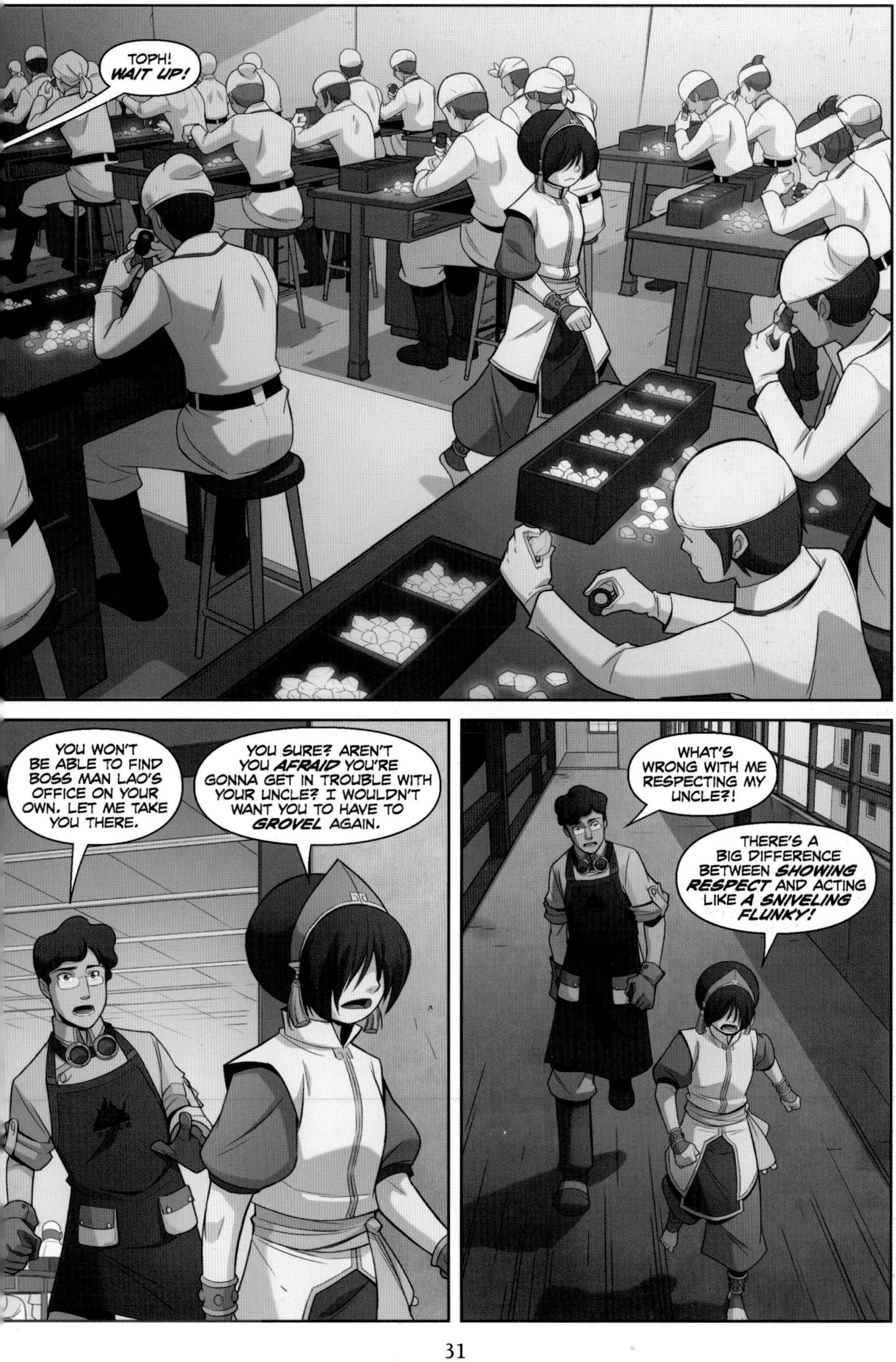
TOPH! WAIT UP!
YOU WON'T BE ABLE TO FIND BOSS MAN LAO'S OFFICE ON YOUR OWN. LET ME TAKE YOU THERE.
YOU SURE? AREN'T YOU AFRAID YOU'RE GONNA GET IN TROUBLE WITH YOUR UNCLE? I WOULDN'T WANT YOU TO HAVE TO GROVEL AGAIN.
WHAT'S WRONG WITH ME RESPECTING MY UNCLE?!
THERE'S A BIG DIFFERENCE BETWEEN SHOWING RESPECT AND ACTING LIKE A SNIVELING FLUNKY!

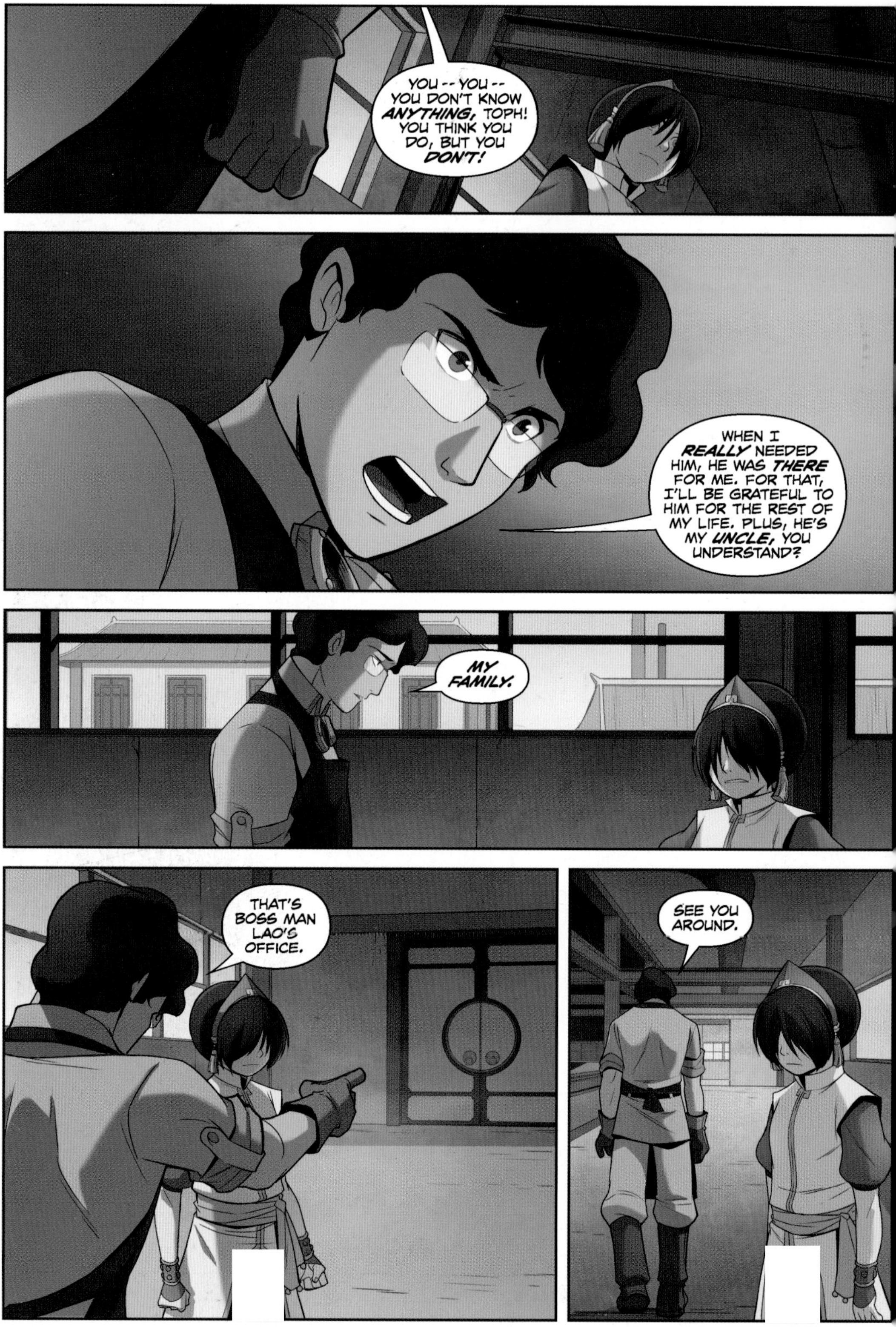
YOU -- YOU -- YOU DON'T KNOW ANYTHING, TOPH! YOU THINK YOU DO, BUT YOU DON'T!
WHEN I REALLY NEEDED HIM, HE WAS THERE FOR ME. FOR THAT, I'LL BE GRATEFUL TO HIM FOR THE REST OF MY LIFE. PLUS, HE'S MY UNCLE, YOU UNDERSTAND?
MY FAMILY.
THAT'S BOSS MAN LAO'S OFFICE.
SEE YOU AROUND.

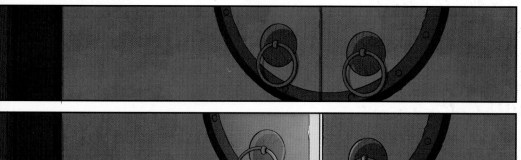

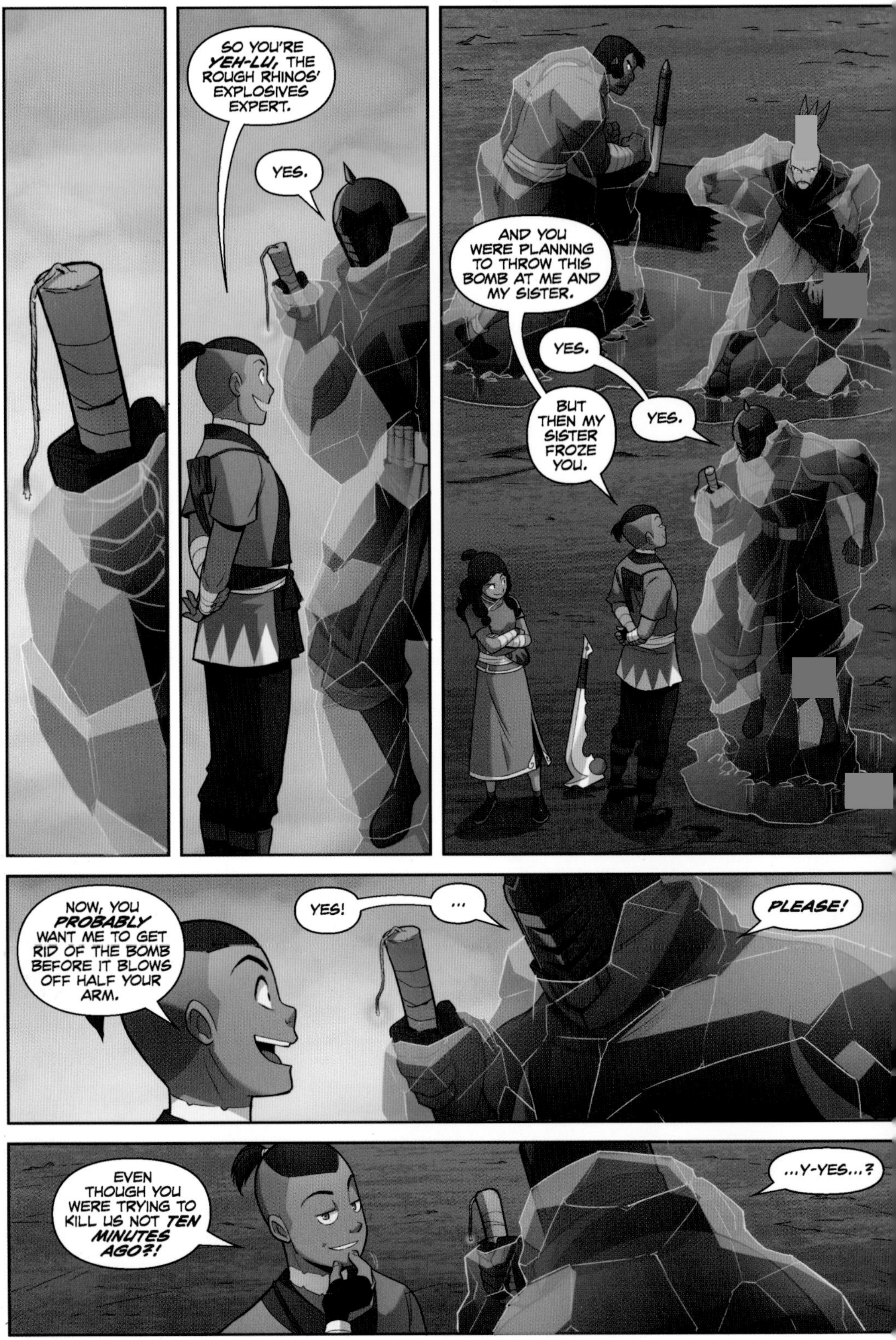
SO YOU'RE YEH-LU, THE ROUGH RHINOS' EXPLOSIVES EXPERT.
YES.
AND YOU WERE PLANNING TO THROW THIS BOMB AT ME AND MY SISTER.
YES.
BUT THEN MY SISTER FROZE YOU.
YES.
NOW, YOU PROBABLY WANT ME TO GET RID OF THE BOMB BEFORE IT BLOWS OFF HALF YOUR ARM.
YES!
...
PLEASE!
EVEN THOUGH YOU WERE TRYING TO KILL US NOT TEN MINUTES AGO?!
...Y-YES...?

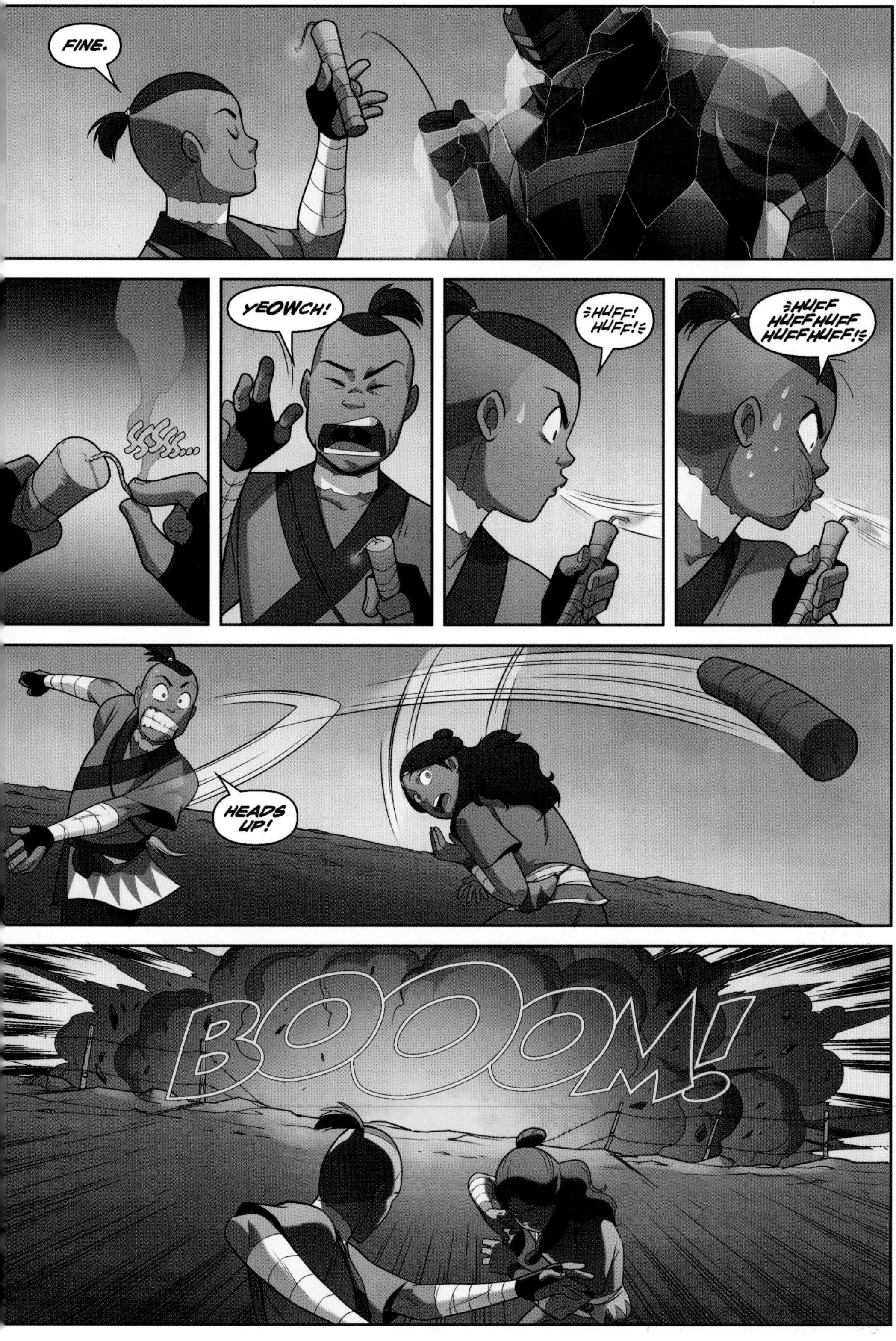
FINE.
SSSSS...
YEOWCH!
HUFF! HUFF!
HUFF HUFFHUFF HUFFHUFF!
HEADS UP!
BOOOM!

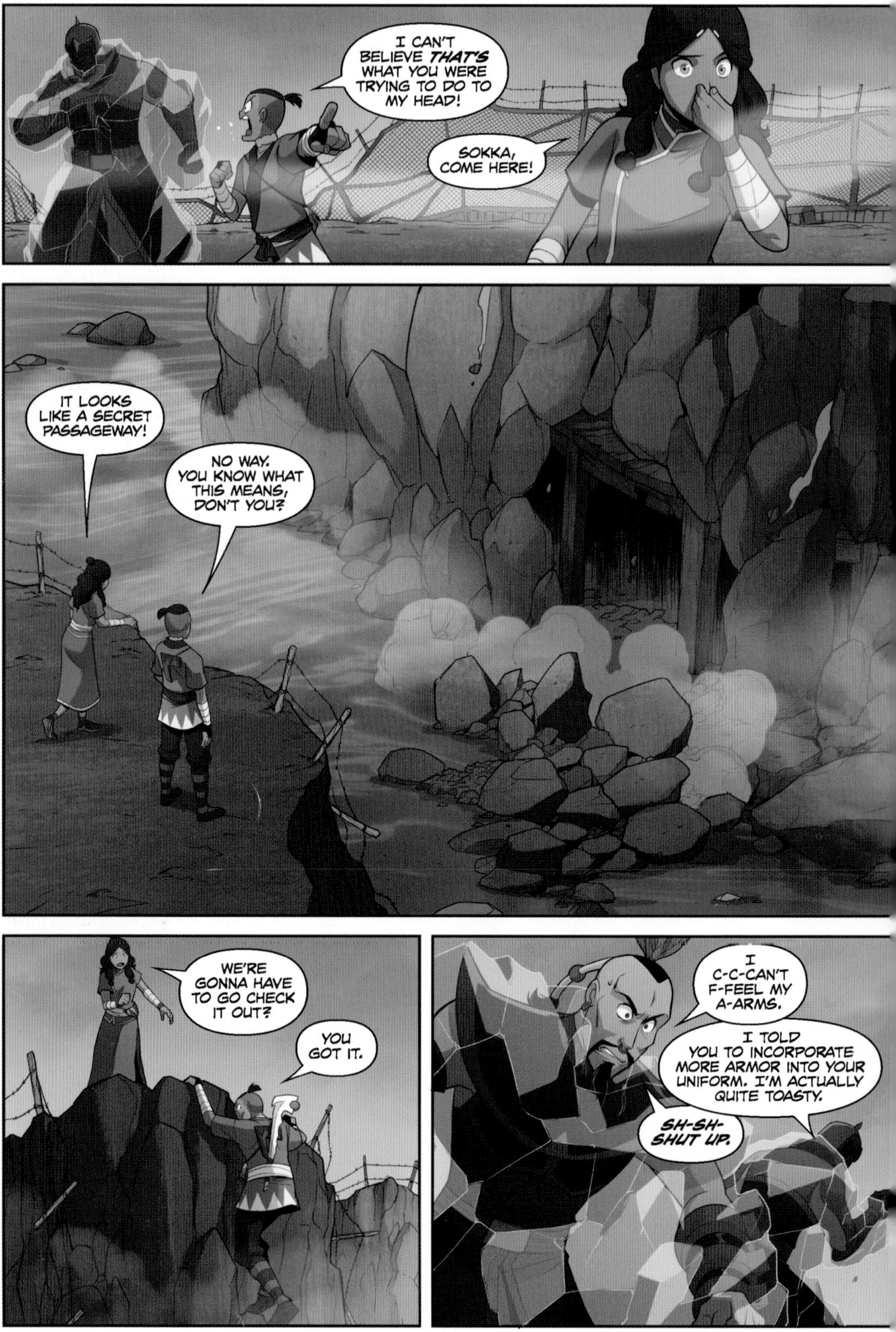
I CAN'T BELIEVE THAT'S WHAT YOU WERE TRYING TO DO TO MY HEAD!
SOKKA, COME HERE!
IT LOOKS LIKE A SECRET PASSAGEWAY!
NO WAY. YOU KNOW WHAT THIS MEANS, DON'T YOU?
WE'RE GONNA HAVE TO GO CHECK IT OUT?
YOU GOT IT.
I C-C-CAN'T F-FEEL MY A-ARMS.
I TOLD YOU TO INCORPORATE MORE ARMOR INTO YOUR UNIFORM. I'M ACTUALLY QUITE TOASTY.
SH-SH-SHUT UP.

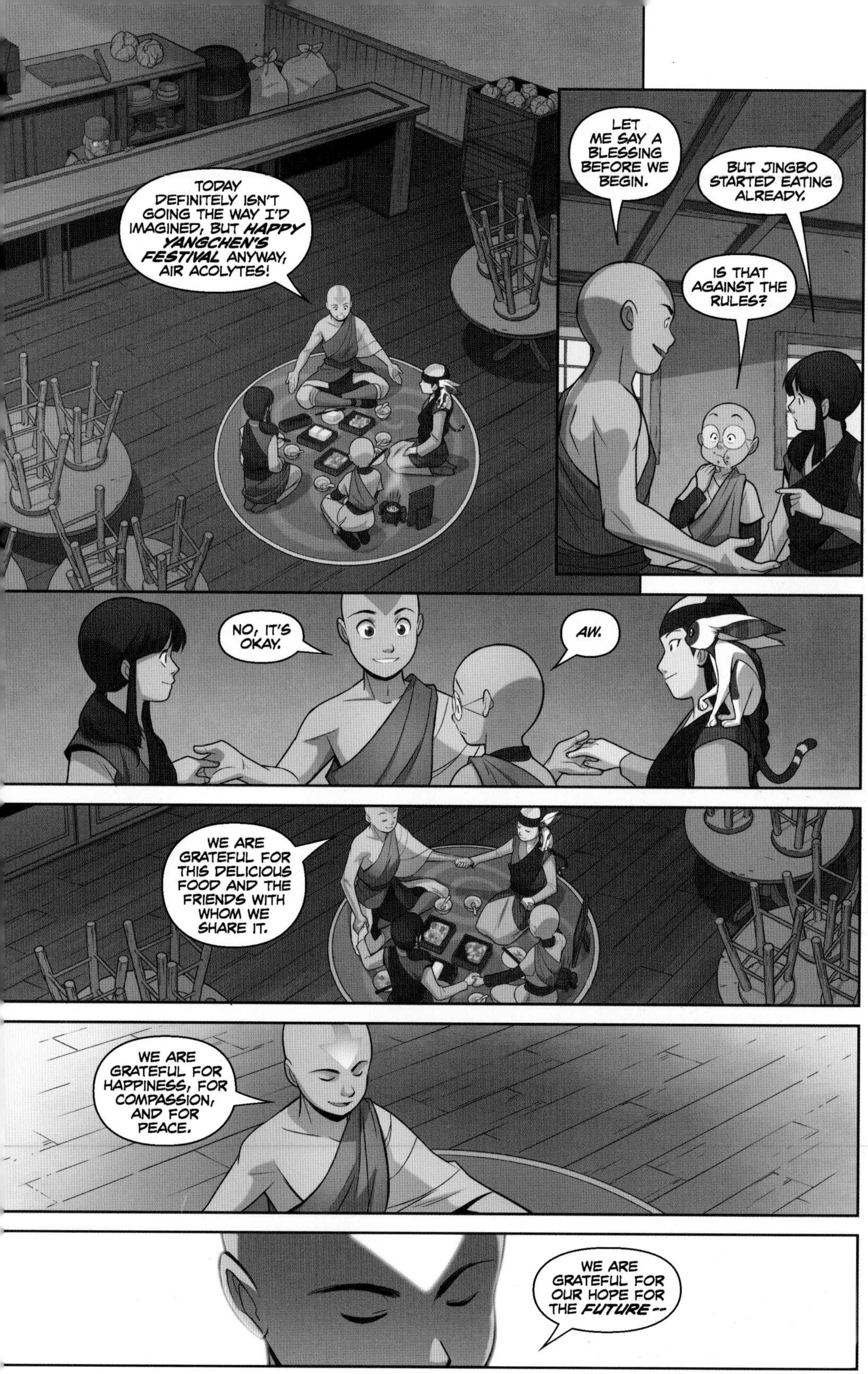
TODAY DEFINITELY ISN'T GOING THE WAY I'D IMAGINED, BUT *HAPPY YANGCHEN'S FESTIVAL* ANYWAY, AIR ACOLYTES!
LET ME SAY A BLESSING BEFORE WE BEGIN.
BUT JINGBO STARTED EATING ALREADY.
IS THAT AGAINST THE RULES?
NO, IT'S OKAY.
AW.
WE ARE GRATEFUL FOR THIS DELICIOUS FOOD AND THE FRIENDS WITH WHOM WE SHARE IT.
WE ARE GRATEFUL FOR HAPPINESS, FOR COMPASSION, AND FOR PEACE.
WE ARE GRATEFUL FOR OUR HOPE FOR THE *FUTURE*--

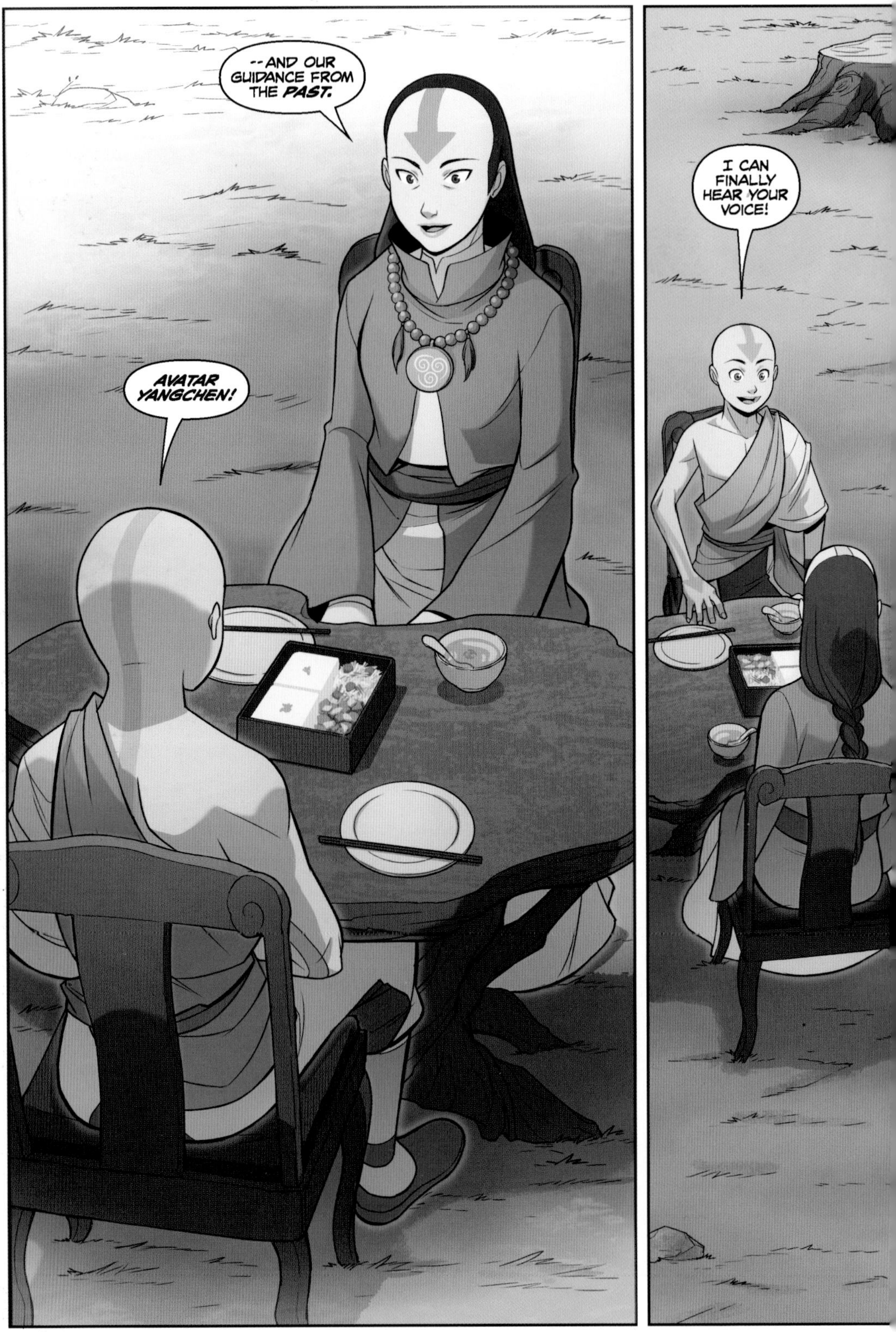
--AND OUR GUIDANCE FROM THE *PAST.*
AVATAR YANGCHEN!
I CAN FINALLY HEAR YOUR VOICE!

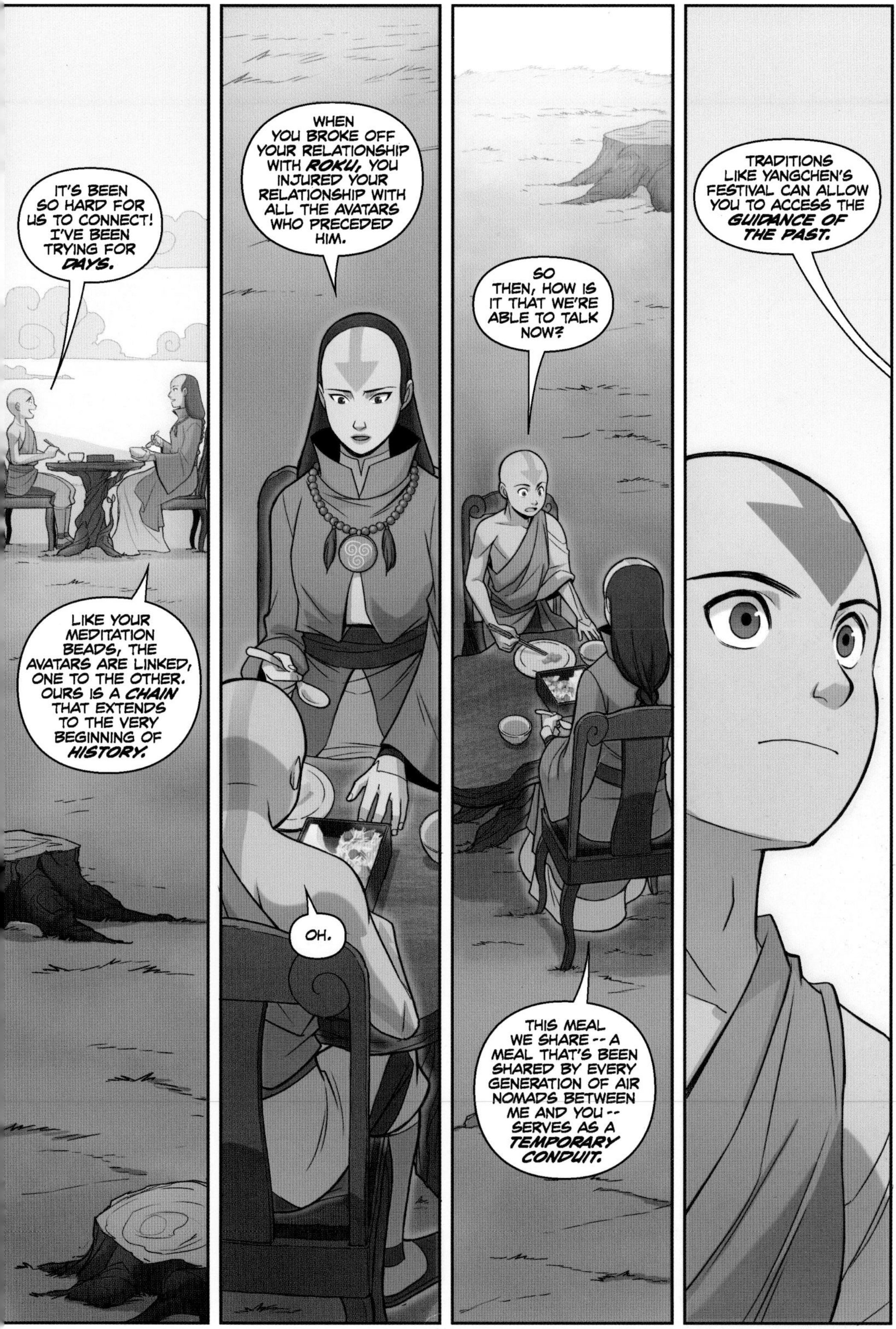
IT'S BEEN SO HARD FOR US TO CONNECT! I'VE BEEN TRYING FOR DAYS.
LIKE YOUR MEDITATION BEADS, THE AVATARS ARE LINKED, ONE TO THE OTHER. OURS IS A CHAIN THAT EXTENDS TO THE VERY BEGINNING OF HISTORY.
WHEN YOU BROKE OFF YOUR RELATIONSHIP WITH ROKU, YOU INJURED YOUR RELATIONSHIP WITH ALL THE AVATARS WHO PRECEDED HIM.
OH.
SO THEN, HOW IS IT THAT WE'RE ABLE TO TALK NOW?
THIS MEAL WE SHARE -- A MEAL THAT'S BEEN SHARED BY EVERY GENERATION OF AIR NOMADS BETWEEN ME AND YOU -- SERVES AS A TEMPORARY CONDUIT.
TRADITIONS LIKE YANGCHEN'S FESTIVAL CAN ALLOW YOU TO ACCESS THE GUIDANCE OF THE PAST.

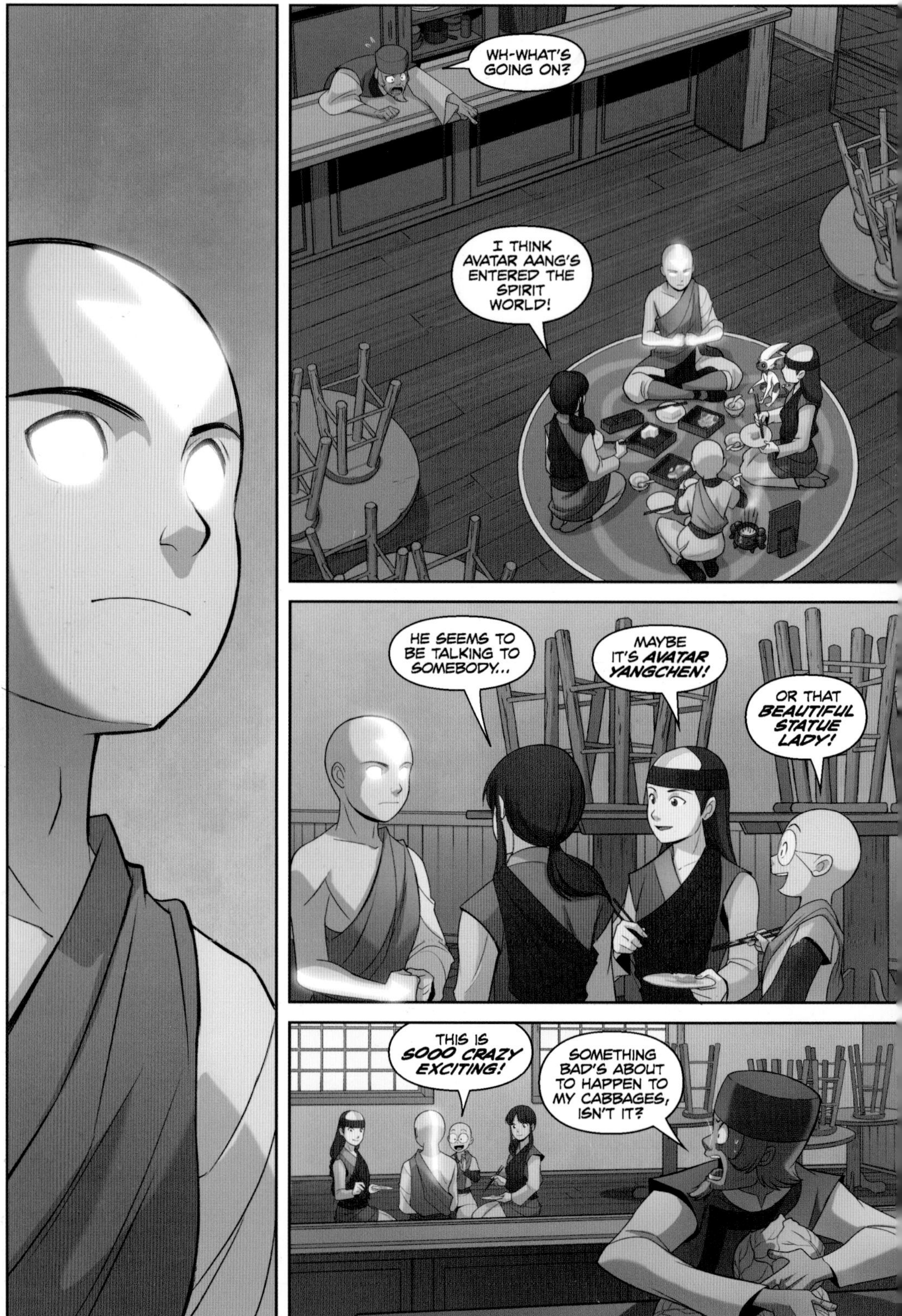
WH-WHAT'S GOING ON?
I THINK AVATAR AANG'S ENTERED THE SPIRIT WORLD!
HE SEEMS TO BE TALKING TO SOMEBODY...
MAYBE IT'S AVATAR YANGCHEN!
OR THAT BEAUTIFUL STATUE LADY!
THIS IS SOOO CRAZY EXCITING!
SOMETHING BAD'S ABOUT TO HAPPEN TO MY CABBAGES, ISN'T IT?

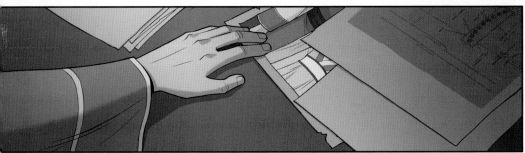

I TOLD YOU ALREADY, YOU'RE *CONFUSED.* YOU ARE *NOT* MY DAUGHTER. NOW SEE YOUR WAY OUT OF HERE BEFORE I CALL SECURITY.

AW, LET IT GO, ALREADY! NOBODY'S HERE BUT YOU AND ME, AND WE BOTH KNOW YOU'RE LYING!

YOU PRESUME TO TELL *ME* WHAT I KNOW?

41

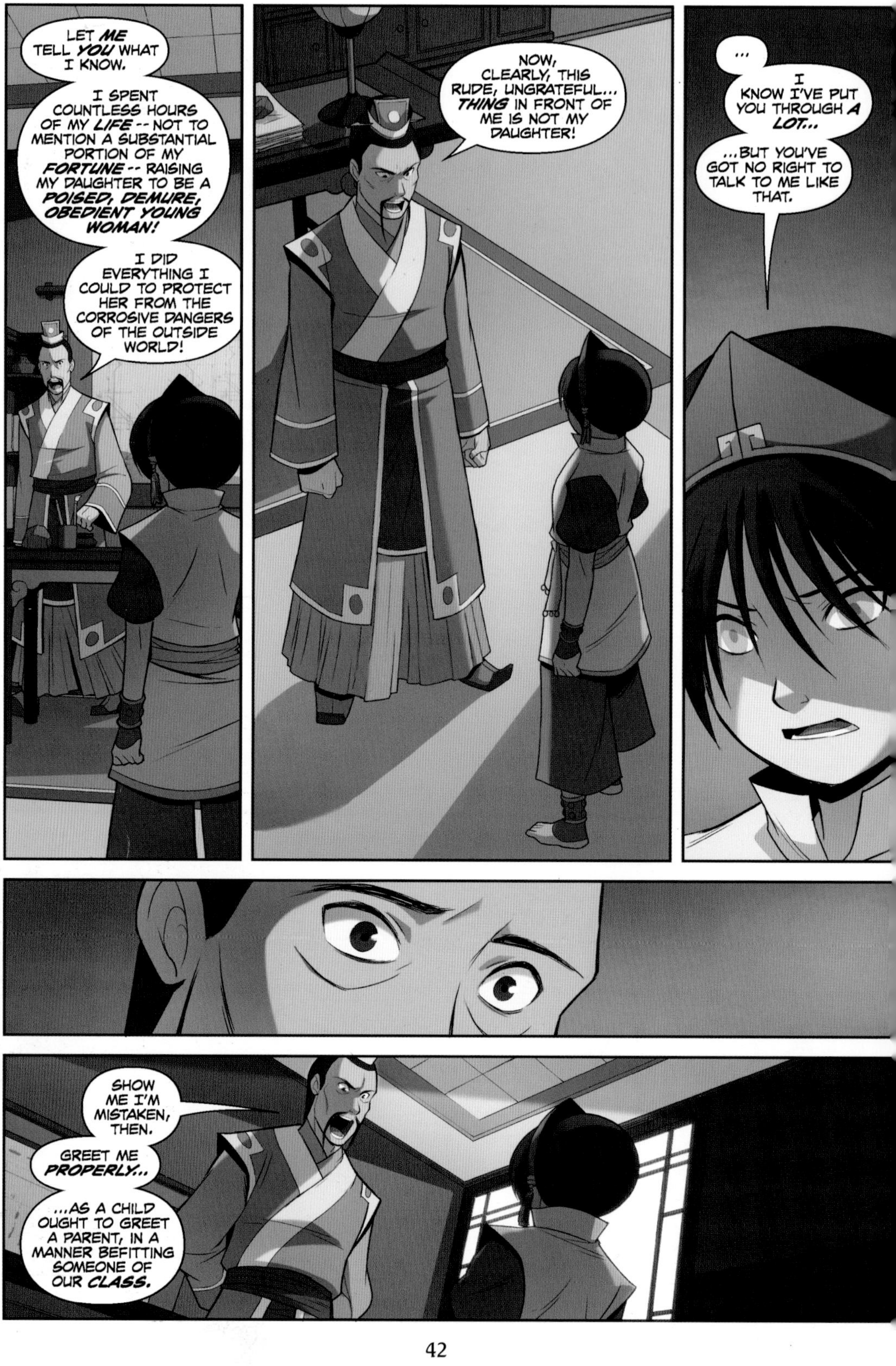
LET ME TELL YOU WHAT I KNOW.
I SPENT COUNTLESS HOURS OF MY LIFE -- NOT TO MENTION A SUBSTANTIAL PORTION OF MY FORTUNE -- RAISING MY DAUGHTER TO BE A POISED, DEMURE, OBEDIENT YOUNG WOMAN!
I DID EVERYTHING I COULD TO PROTECT HER FROM THE CORROSIVE DANGERS OF THE OUTSIDE WORLD!
NOW, CLEARLY, THIS RUDE, UNGRATEFUL... THING IN FRONT OF ME IS NOT MY DAUGHTER!
...
I KNOW I'VE PUT YOU THROUGH A LOT...
...BUT YOU'VE GOT NO RIGHT TO TALK TO ME LIKE THAT.
SHOW ME I'M MISTAKEN, THEN.
GREET ME PROPERLY...
...AS A CHILD OUGHT TO GREET A PARENT, IN A MANNER BEFITTING SOMEONE OF OUR CLASS.

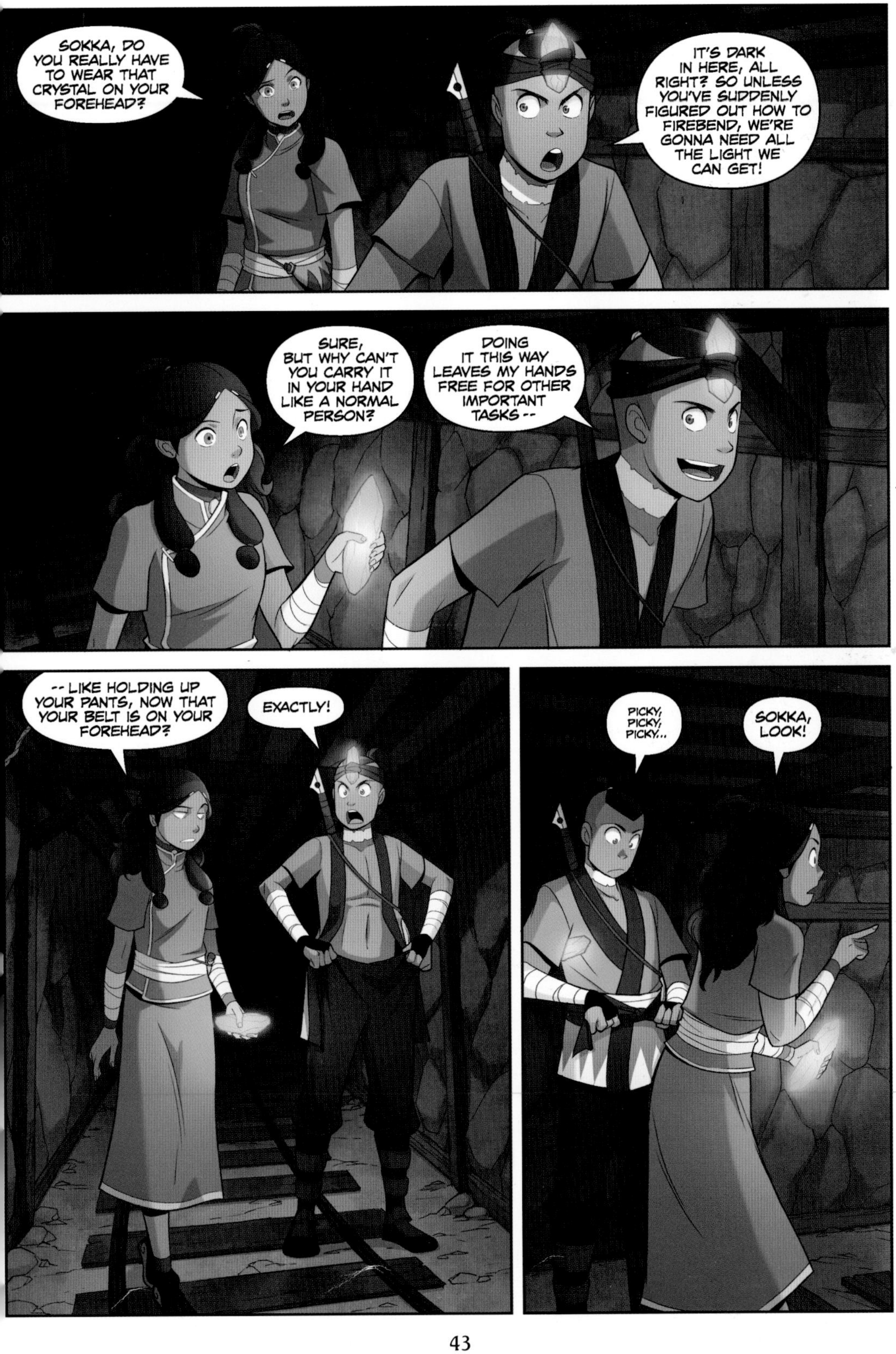
SOKKA, DO YOU REALLY HAVE TO WEAR THAT CRYSTAL ON YOUR FOREHEAD?
IT'S DARK IN HERE, ALL RIGHT? SO UNLESS YOU'VE SUDDENLY FIGURED OUT HOW TO FIREBEND, WE'RE GONNA NEED ALL THE LIGHT WE CAN GET!
SURE, BUT WHY CAN'T YOU CARRY IT IN YOUR HAND LIKE A NORMAL PERSON?
DOING IT THIS WAY LEAVES MY HANDS FREE FOR OTHER IMPORTANT TASKS --
-- LIKE HOLDING UP YOUR PANTS, NOW THAT YOUR BELT IS ON YOUR FOREHEAD?
EXACTLY!
PICKY, PICKY, PICKY...
SOKKA, LOOK!

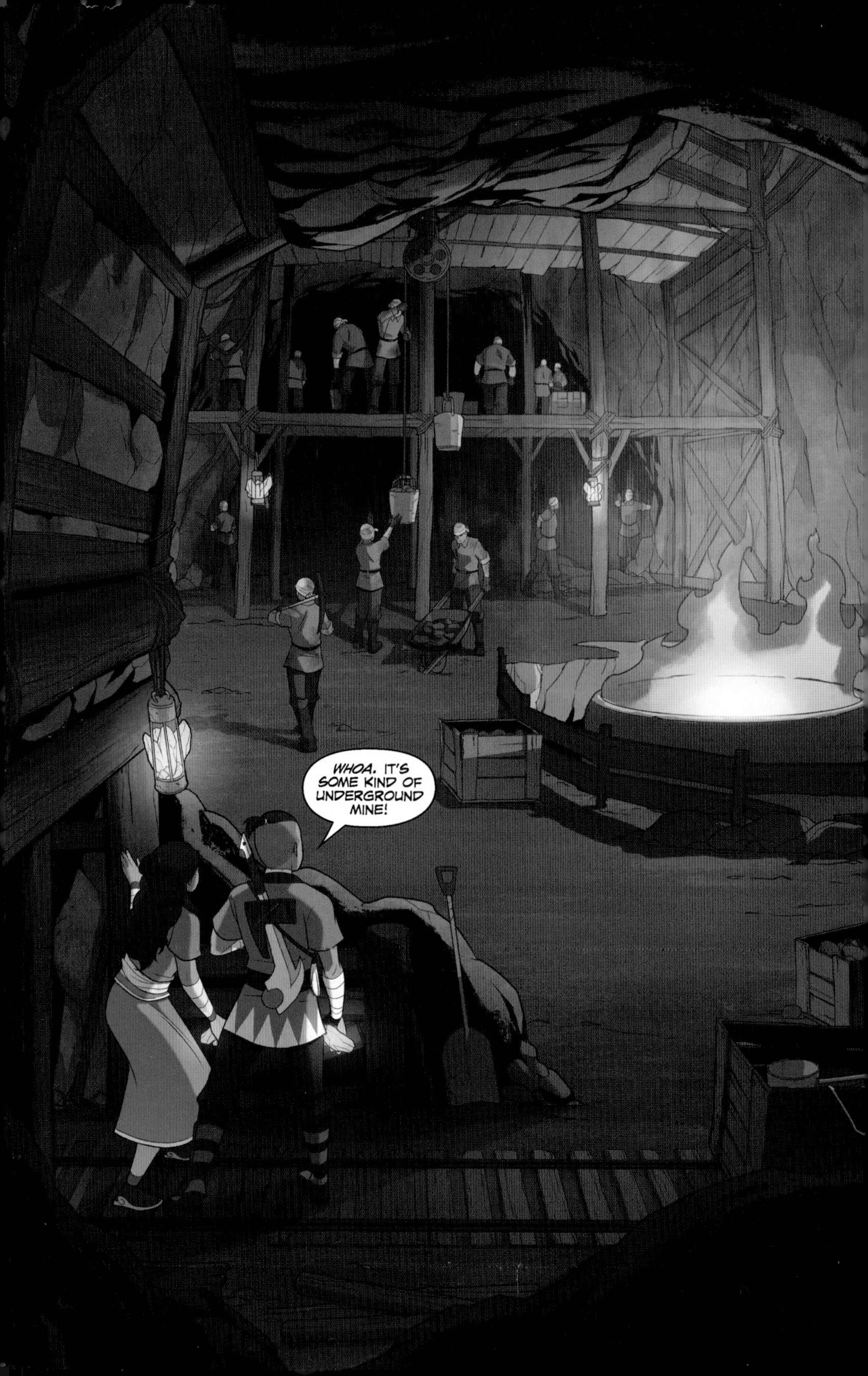
WHOA. IT'S SOME KIND OF UNDERGROUND MINE!

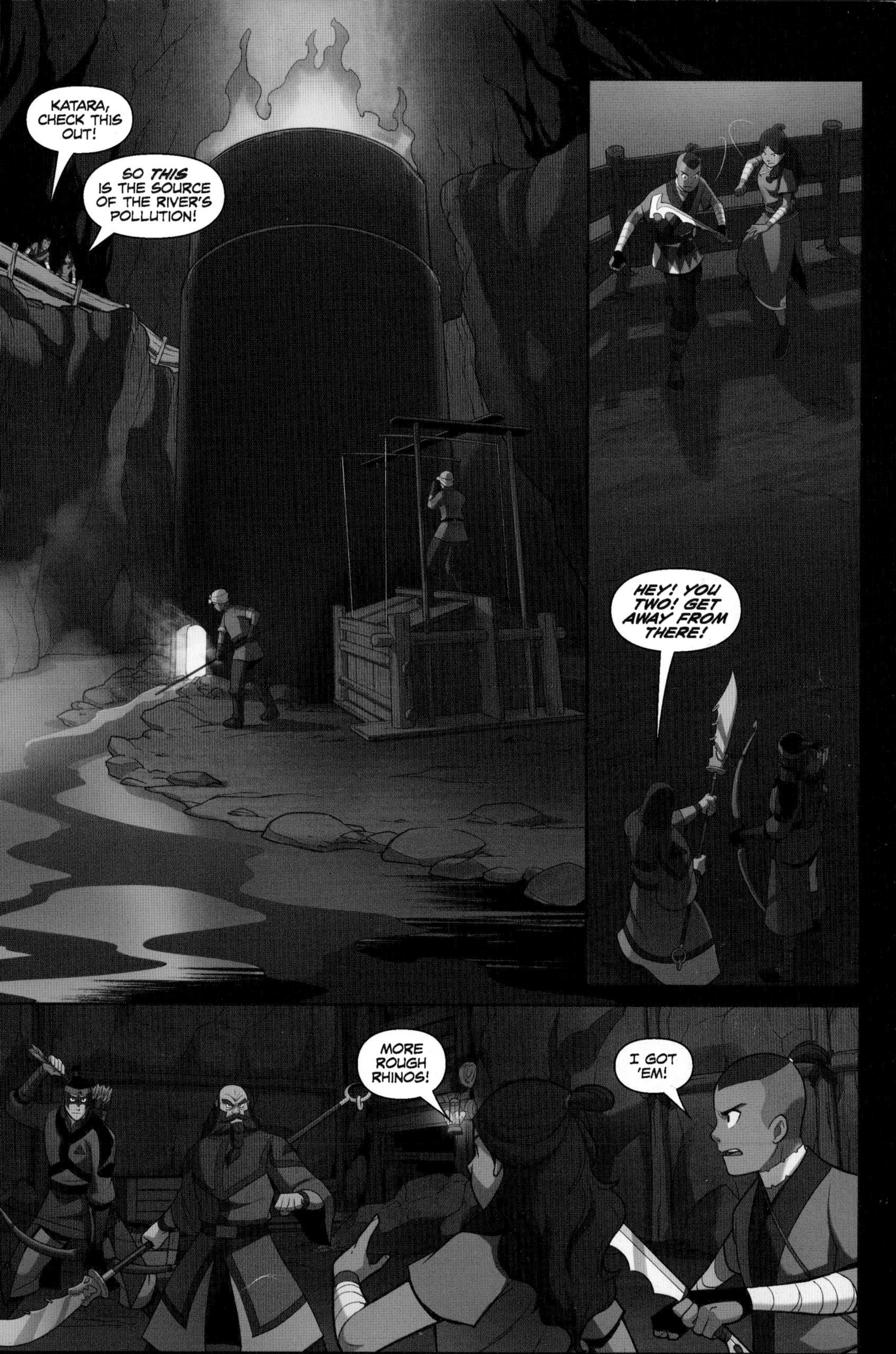
KATARA, CHECK THIS OUT!
SO *THIS* IS THE SOURCE OF THE RIVER'S POLLUTION!
HEY! YOU TWO! GET AWAY FROM THERE!
MORE ROUGH RHINOS!
I GOT 'EM!

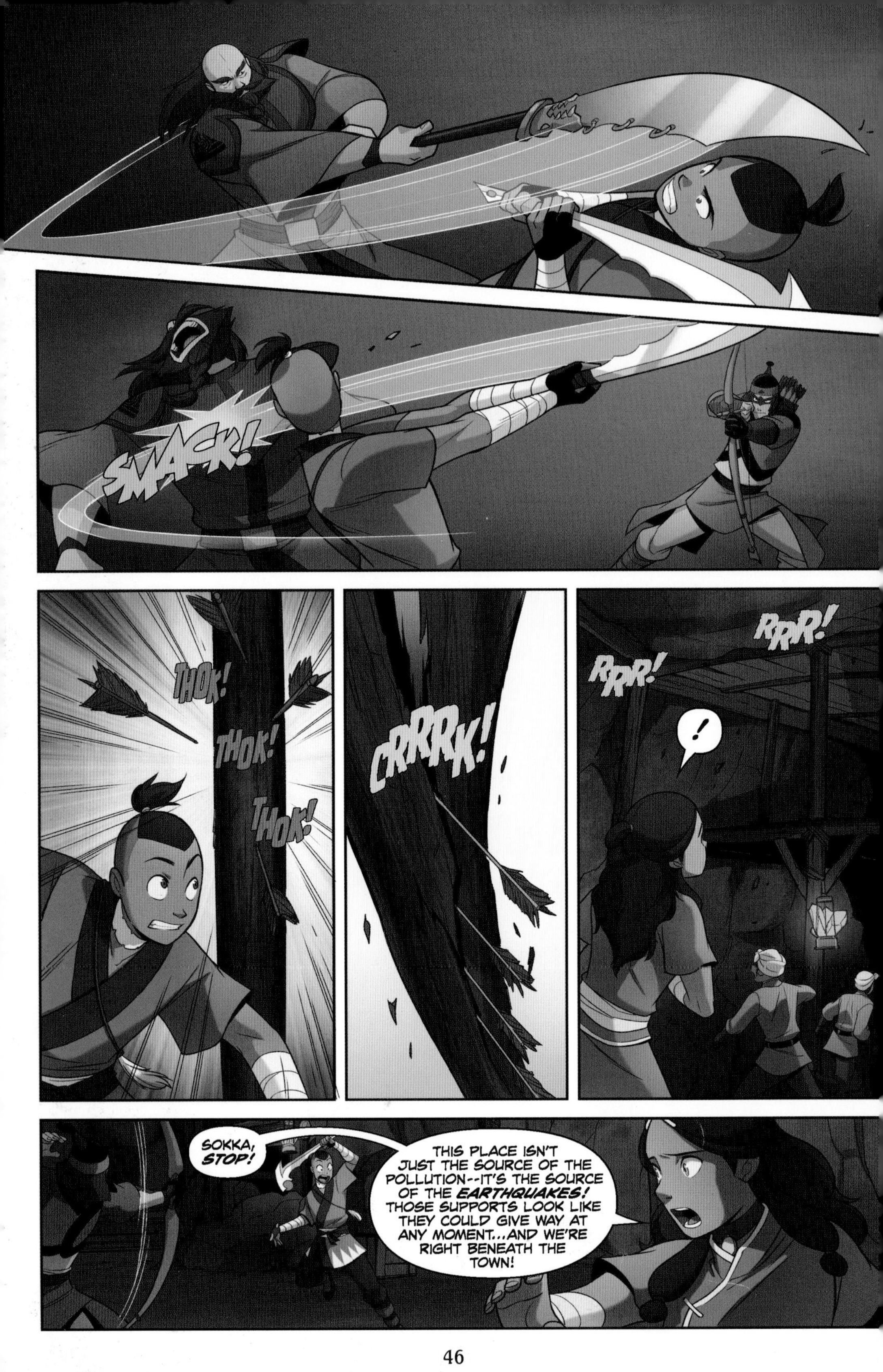
SMACK!
THOK!
THOK!
THOK!
CRRRK!
RRR!
RRR!
!
SOKKA, STOP!
THIS PLACE ISN'T JUST THE SOURCE OF THE POLLUTION--IT'S THE SOURCE OF THE EARTHQUAKES! THOSE SUPPORTS LOOK LIKE THEY COULD GIVE WAY AT ANY MOMENT...AND WE'RE RIGHT BENEATH THE TOWN!

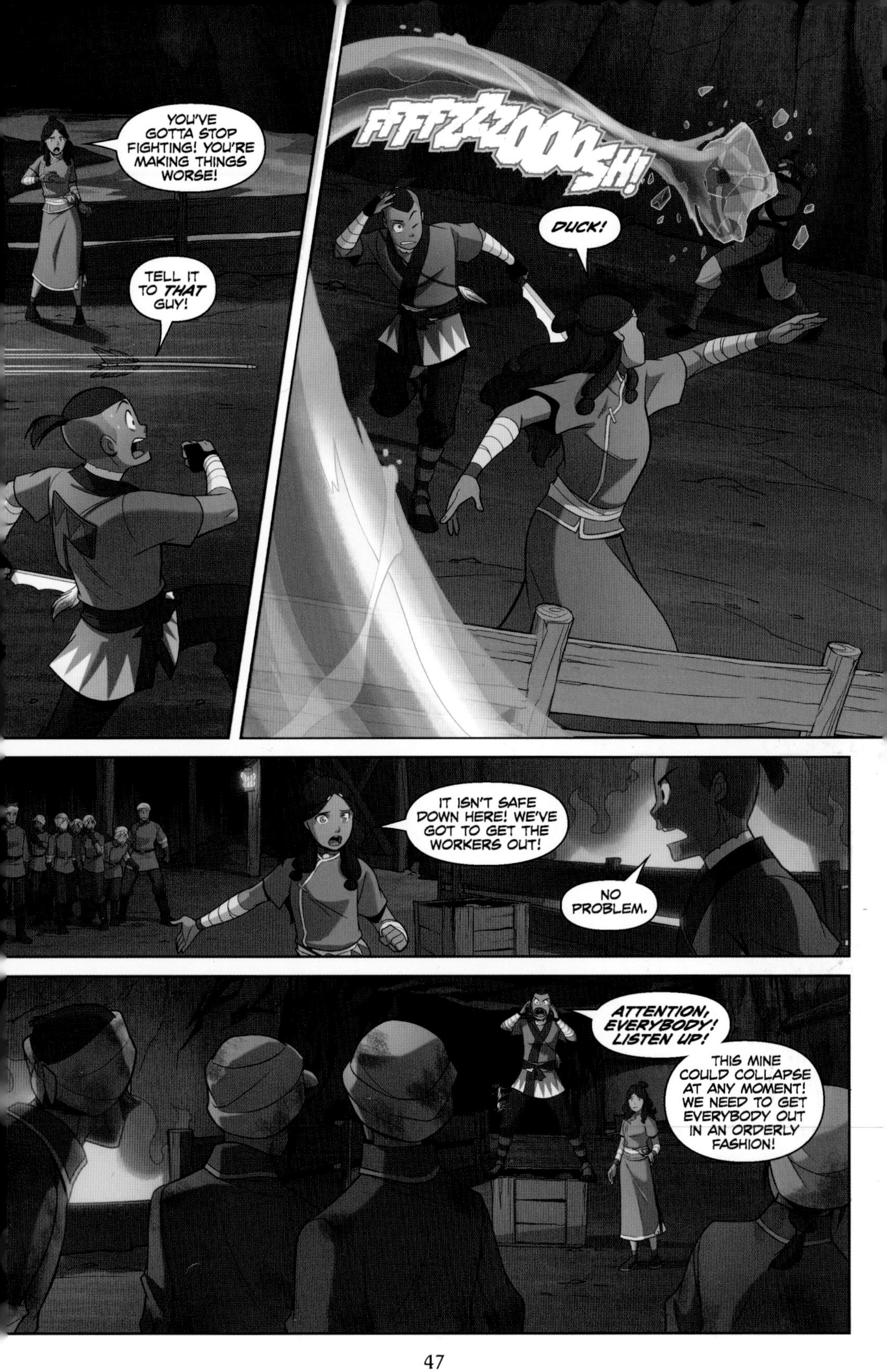
YOU'VE GOTTA STOP FIGHTING! YOU'RE MAKING THINGS WORSE!
TELL IT TO *THAT* GUY!
FFFZZZOOOOSH!
DUCK!
IT ISN'T SAFE DOWN HERE! WE'VE GOT TO GET THE WORKERS OUT!
NO PROBLEM.
ATTENTION, EVERYBODY! LISTEN UP!
THIS MINE COULD COLLAPSE AT ANY MOMENT! WE NEED TO GET EVERYBODY OUT IN AN ORDERLY FASHION!

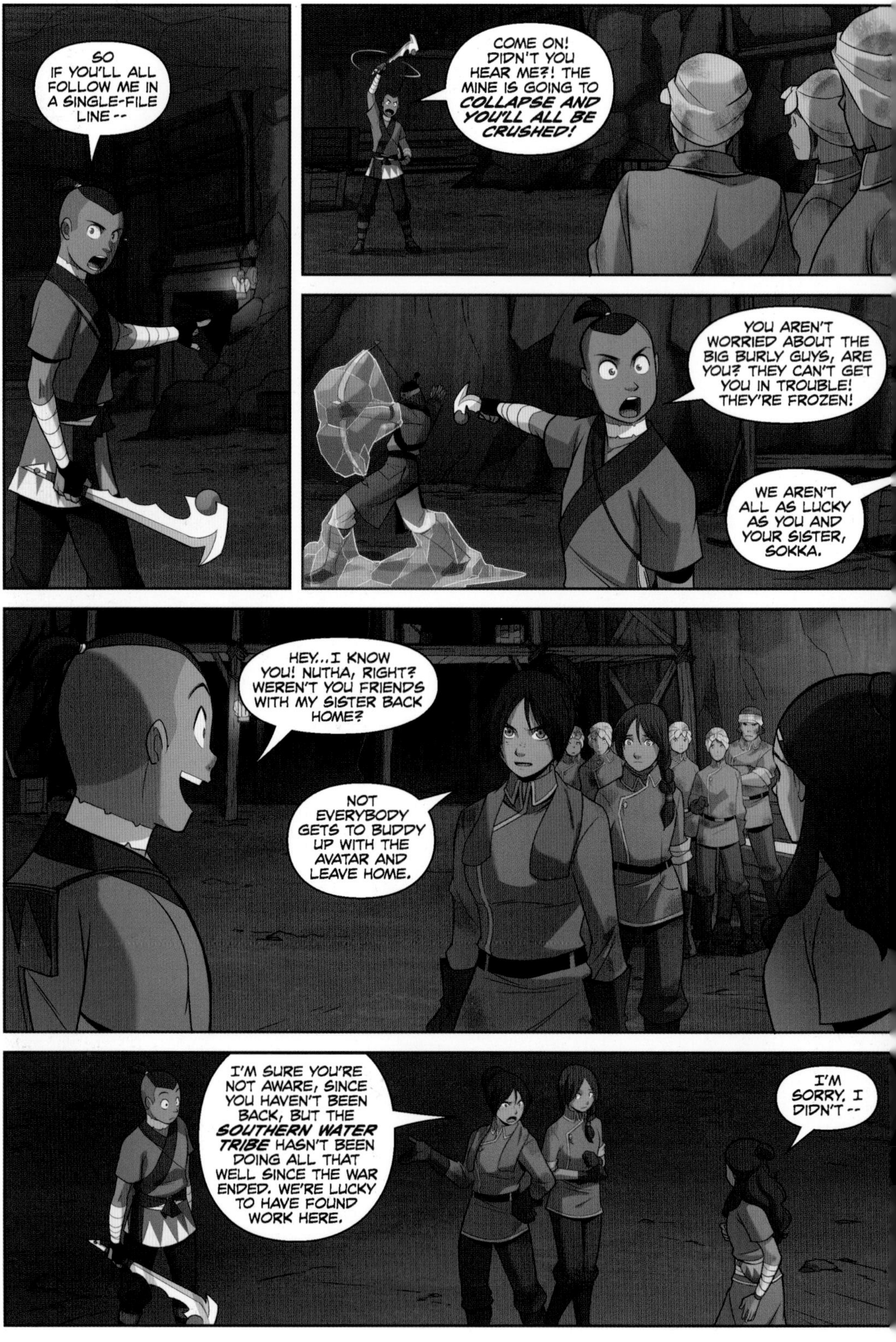
SO IF YOU'LL ALL FOLLOW ME IN A SINGLE-FILE LINE --
COME ON! DIDN'T YOU HEAR ME?! THE MINE IS GOING TO COLLAPSE AND YOU'LL ALL BE CRUSHED!
YOU AREN'T WORRIED ABOUT THE BIG BURLY GUYS, ARE YOU? THEY CAN'T GET YOU IN TROUBLE! THEY'RE FROZEN!
WE AREN'T ALL AS LUCKY AS YOU AND YOUR SISTER, SOKKA.
HEY...I KNOW YOU! NUTHA, RIGHT? WEREN'T YOU FRIENDS WITH MY SISTER BACK HOME?
NOT EVERYBODY GETS TO BUDDY UP WITH THE AVATAR AND LEAVE HOME.
I'M SURE YOU'RE NOT AWARE, SINCE YOU HAVEN'T BEEN BACK, BUT THE SOUTHERN WATER TRIBE HASN'T BEEN DOING ALL THAT WELL SINCE THE WAR ENDED. WE'RE LUCKY TO HAVE FOUND WORK HERE.
I'M SORRY. I DIDN'T --

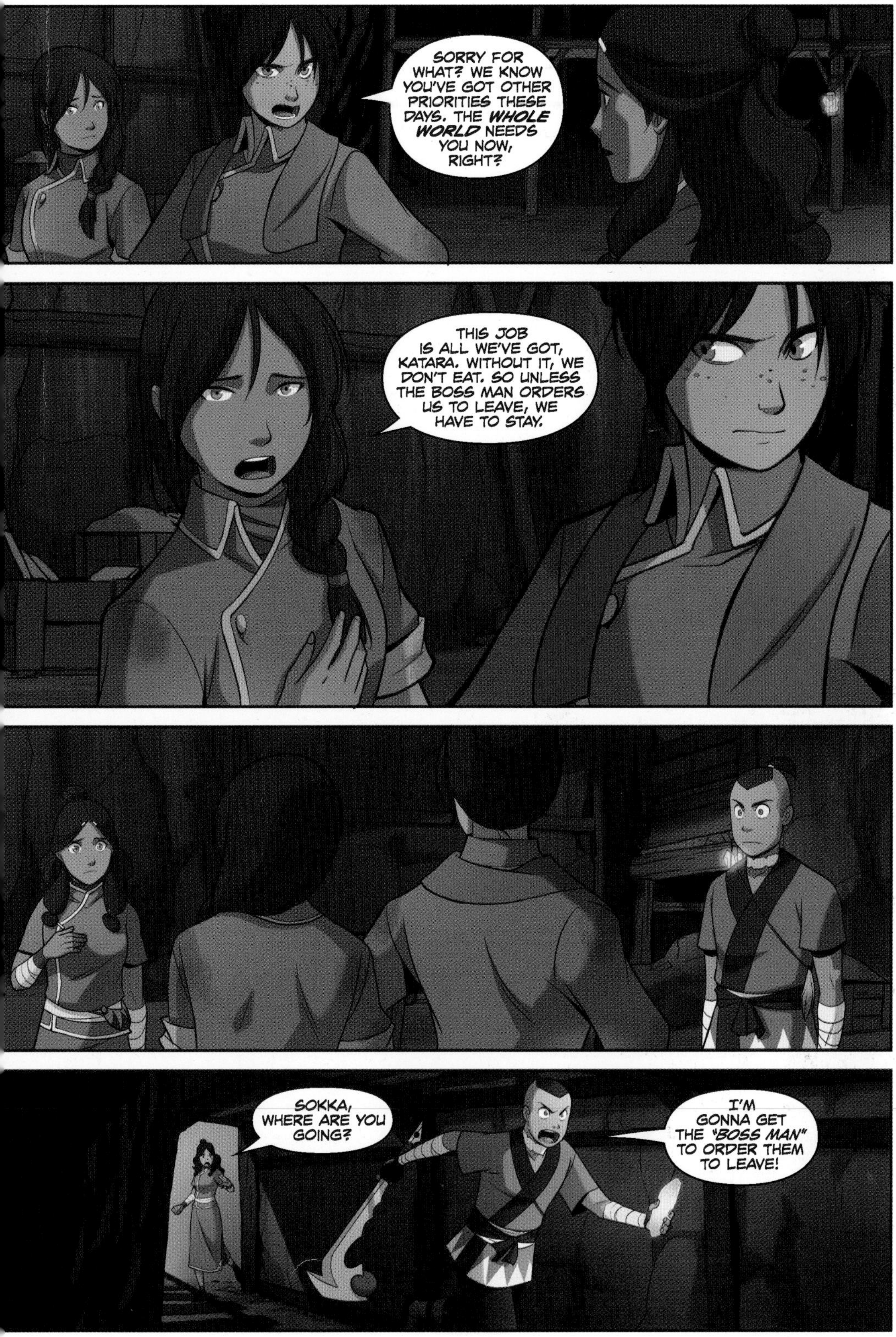
SORRY FOR WHAT? WE KNOW YOU'VE GOT OTHER PRIORITIES THESE DAYS. THE WHOLE WORLD NEEDS YOU NOW, RIGHT?
THIS JOB IS ALL WE'VE GOT, KATARA. WITHOUT IT, WE DON'T EAT. SO UNLESS THE BOSS MAN ORDERS US TO LEAVE, WE HAVE TO STAY.
SOKKA, WHERE ARE YOU GOING?
I'M GONNA GET THE "BOSS MAN" TO ORDER THEM TO LEAVE!

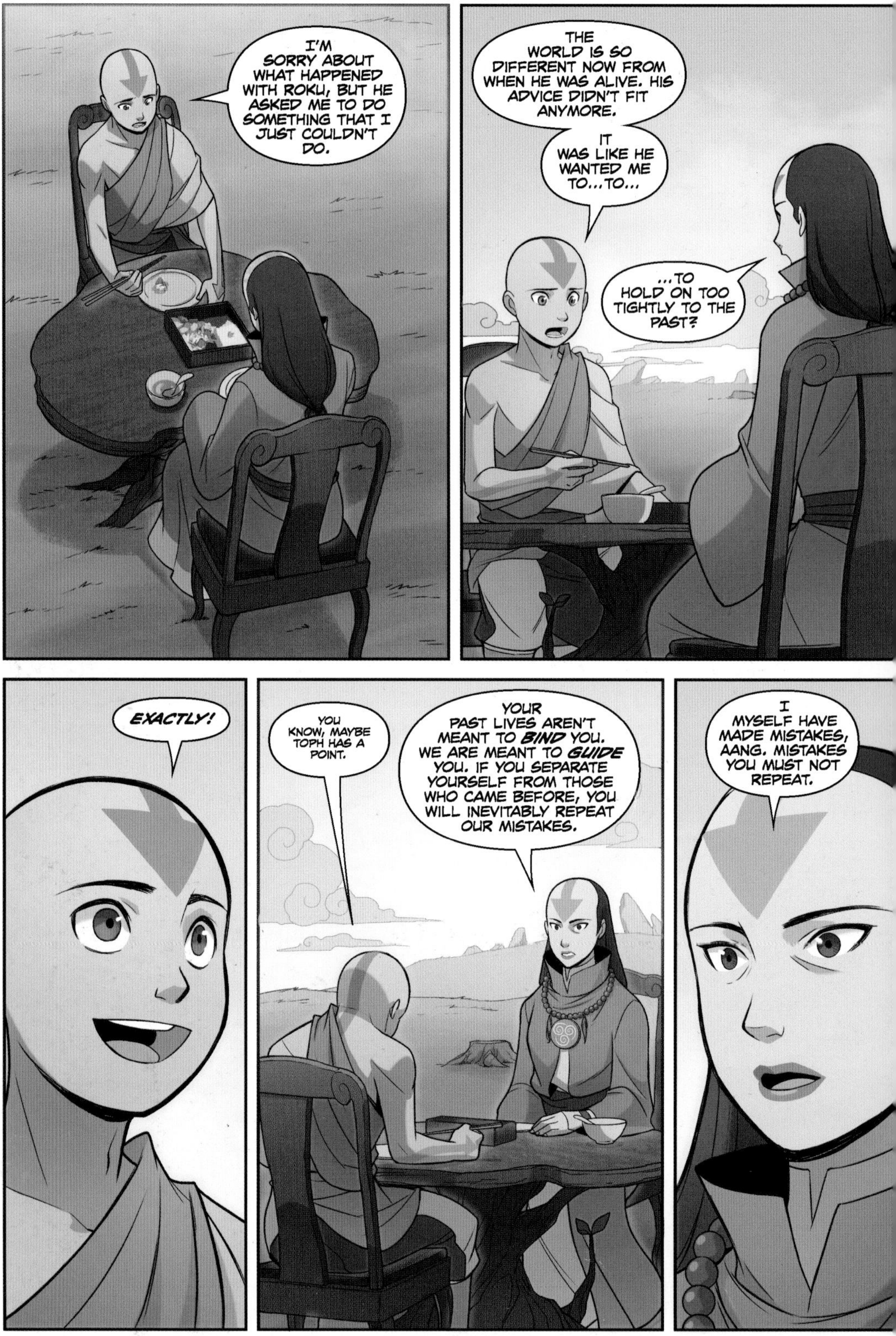
I'M SORRY ABOUT WHAT HAPPENED WITH ROKU, BUT HE ASKED ME TO DO SOMETHING THAT I JUST COULDN'T DO.
THE WORLD IS SO DIFFERENT NOW FROM WHEN HE WAS ALIVE. HIS ADVICE DIDN'T FIT ANYMORE.
IT WAS LIKE HE WANTED ME TO...TO...
...TO HOLD ON TOO TIGHTLY TO THE PAST?
EXACTLY!
YOU KNOW, MAYBE TOPH HAS A POINT.
YOUR PAST LIVES AREN'T MEANT TO BIND YOU. WE ARE MEANT TO GUIDE YOU. IF YOU SEPARATE YOURSELF FROM THOSE WHO CAME BEFORE, YOU WILL INEVITABLY REPEAT OUR MISTAKES.
I MYSELF HAVE MADE MISTAKES, AANG. MISTAKES YOU MUST NOT REPEAT.

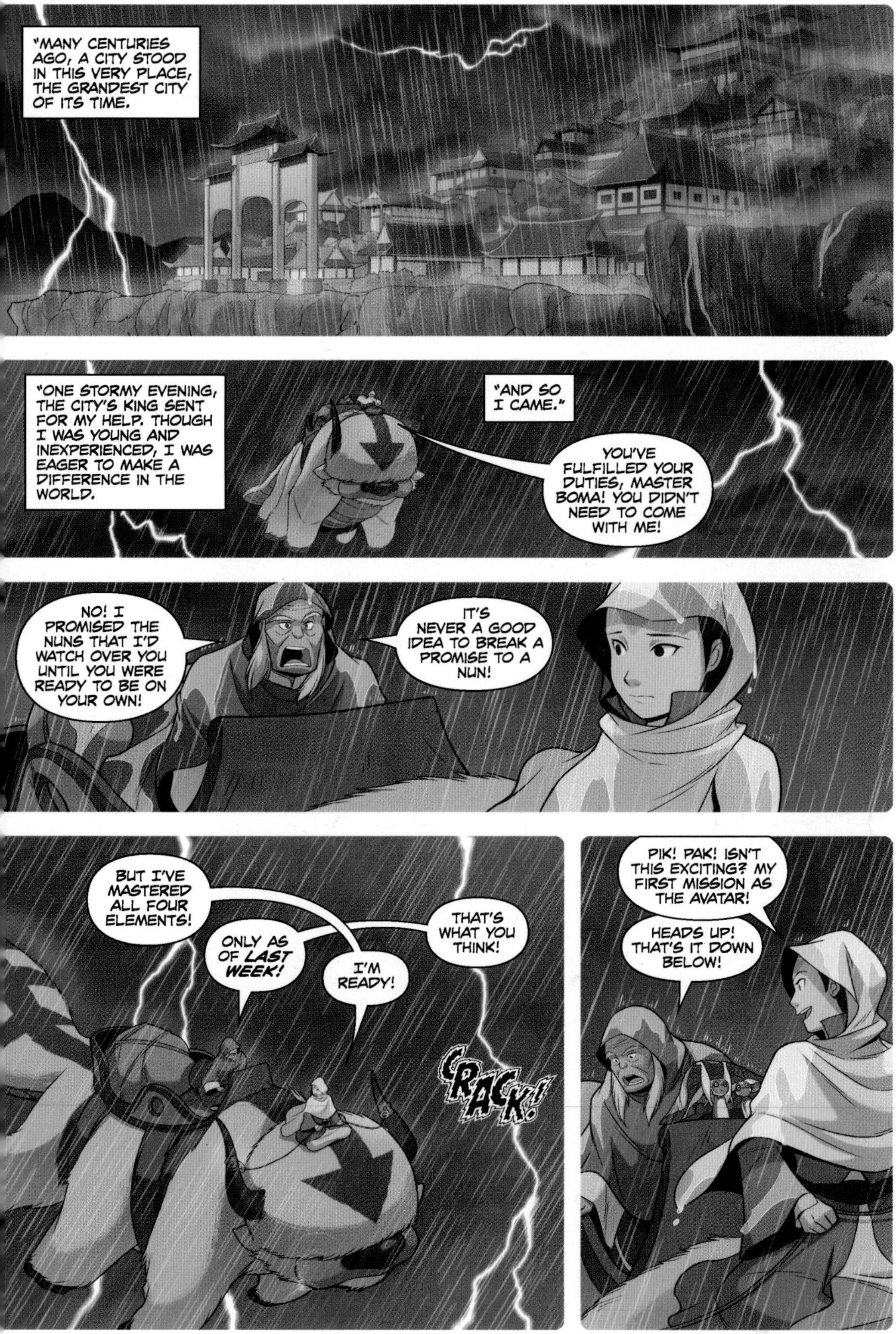
"MANY CENTURIES AGO, A CITY STOOD IN THIS VERY PLACE, THE GRANDEST CITY OF ITS TIME.
"ONE STORMY EVENING, THE CITY'S KING SENT FOR MY HELP. THOUGH I WAS YOUNG AND INEXPERIENCED, I WAS EAGER TO MAKE A DIFFERENCE IN THE WORLD.
"AND SO I CAME."
YOU'VE FULFILLED YOUR DUTIES, MASTER BOMA! YOU DIDN'T NEED TO COME WITH ME!
NO! I PROMISED THE NUNS THAT I'D WATCH OVER YOU UNTIL YOU WERE READY TO BE ON YOUR OWN!
IT'S NEVER A GOOD IDEA TO BREAK A PROMISE TO A NUN!
BUT I'VE MASTERED ALL FOUR ELEMENTS!
ONLY AS OF *LAST WEEK!*
THAT'S WHAT YOU THINK!
I'M READY!
CRACK!
PIK! PAK! ISN'T THIS EXCITING? MY FIRST MISSION AS THE AVATAR!
HEADS UP! THAT'S IT DOWN BELOW!

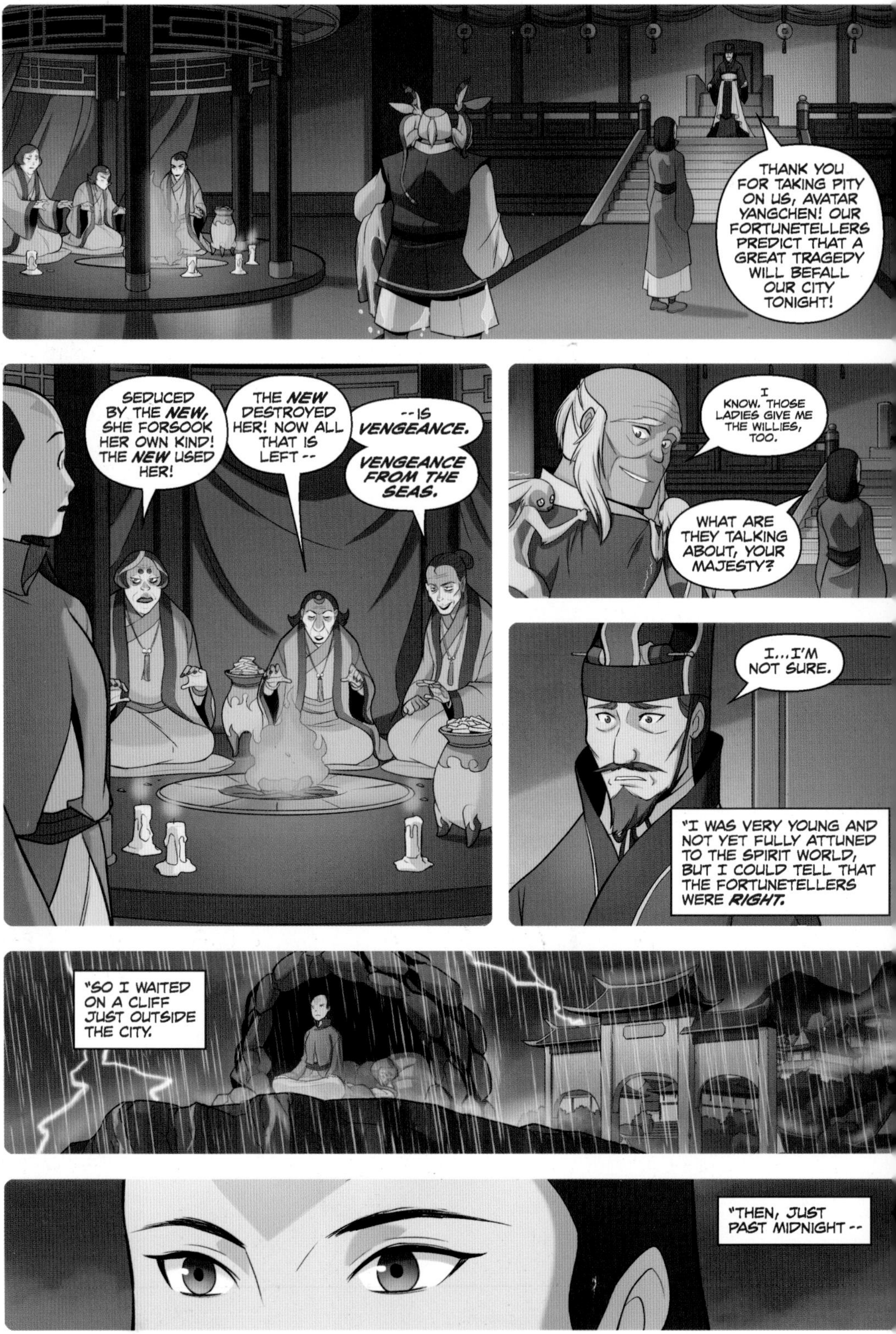
THANK YOU FOR TAKING PITY ON US, AVATAR YANGCHEN! OUR FORTUNETELLERS PREDICT THAT A GREAT TRAGEDY WILL BEFALL OUR CITY TONIGHT!
SEDUCED BY THE NEW, SHE FORSOOK HER OWN KIND! THE NEW USED HER!
THE NEW DESTROYED HER! NOW ALL THAT IS LEFT --
--IS VENGEANCE.
VENGEANCE FROM THE SEAS.
I KNOW. THOSE LADIES GIVE ME THE WILLIES, TOO.
WHAT ARE THEY TALKING ABOUT, YOUR MAJESTY?
I...I'M NOT SURE.
"I WAS VERY YOUNG AND NOT YET FULLY ATTUNED TO THE SPIRIT WORLD, BUT I COULD TELL THAT THE FORTUNETELLERS WERE RIGHT.
"SO I WAITED ON A CLIFF JUST OUTSIDE THE CITY.
"THEN, JUST PAST MIDNIGHT --

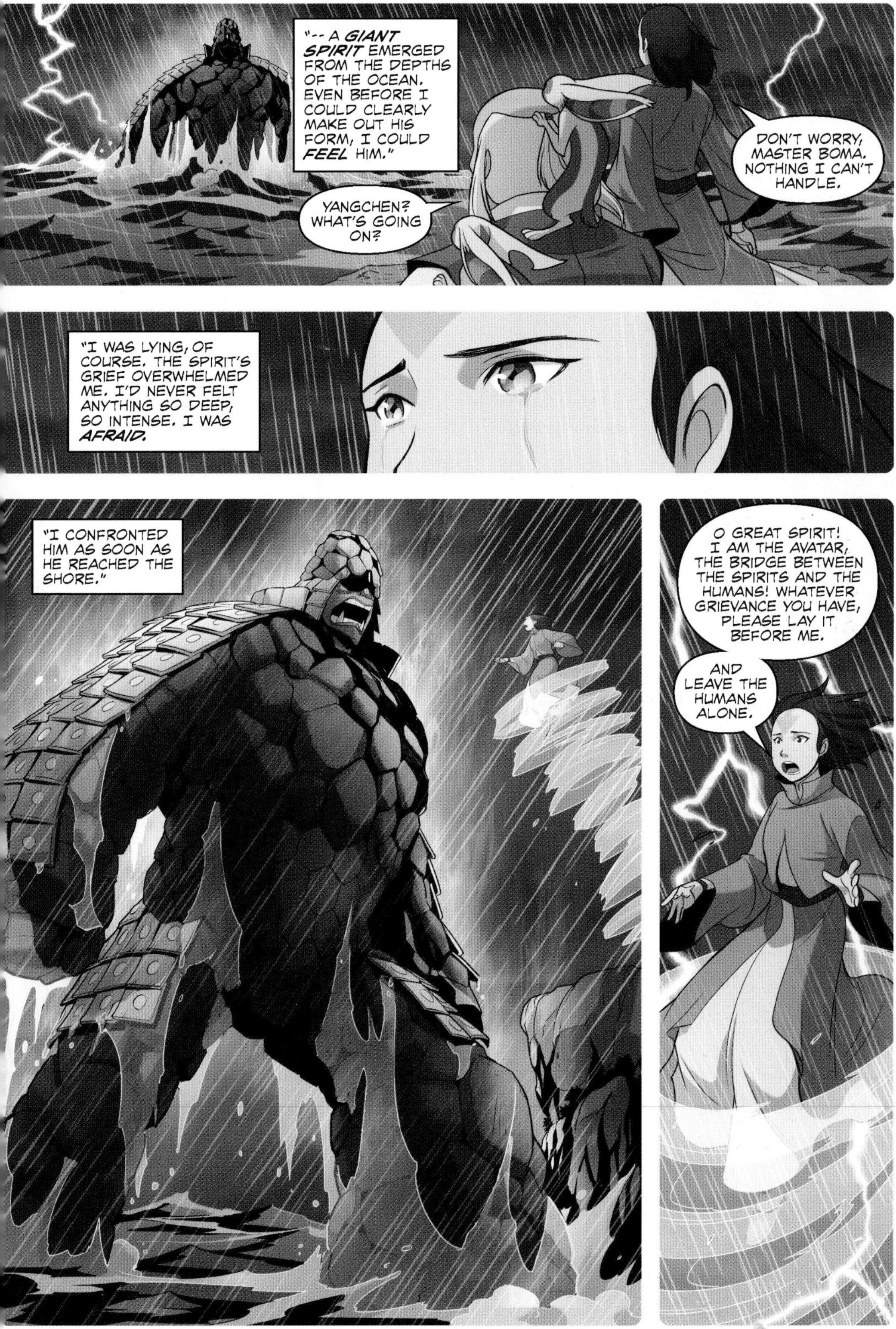
"-- A GIANT SPIRIT EMERGED FROM THE DEPTHS OF THE OCEAN. EVEN BEFORE I COULD CLEARLY MAKE OUT HIS FORM, I COULD FEEL HIM."
YANGCHEN? WHAT'S GOING ON?
DON'T WORRY, MASTER BOMA. NOTHING I CAN'T HANDLE.
"I WAS LYING, OF COURSE. THE SPIRIT'S GRIEF OVERWHELMED ME. I'D NEVER FELT ANYTHING SO DEEP, SO INTENSE. I WAS AFRAID.
"I CONFRONTED HIM AS SOON AS HE REACHED THE SHORE."
O GREAT SPIRIT! I AM THE AVATAR, THE BRIDGE BETWEEN THE SPIRITS AND THE HUMANS! WHATEVER GRIEVANCE YOU HAVE, PLEASE LAY IT BEFORE ME.
AND LEAVE THE HUMANS ALONE.

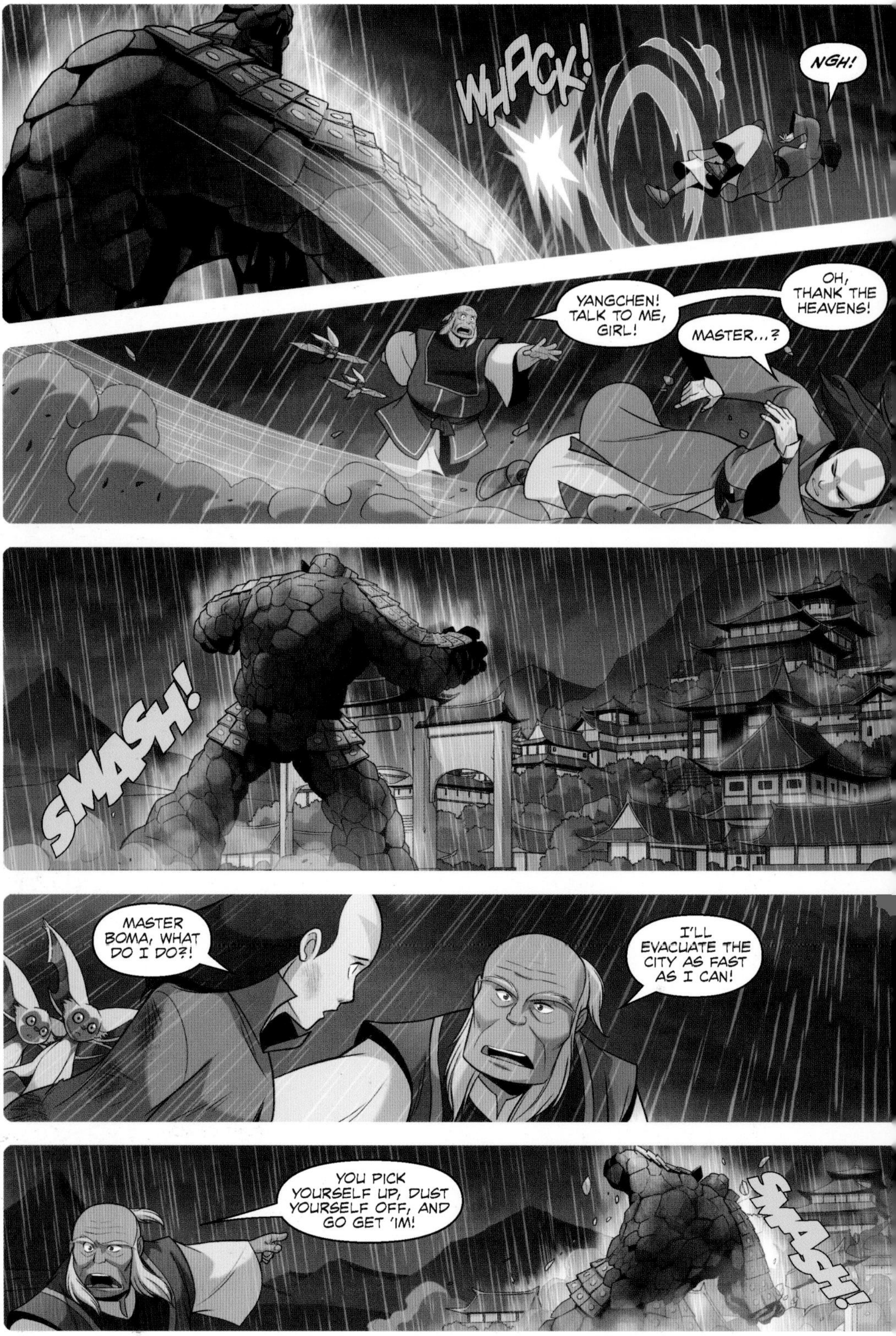
WHACK!
NGH!
YANGCHEN! TALK TO ME, GIRL!
MASTER...?
OH, THANK THE HEAVENS!
SMASH!
MASTER BOMA, WHAT DO I DO?!
I'LL EVACUATE THE CITY AS FAST AS I CAN!
YOU PICK YOURSELF UP, DUST YOURSELF OFF, AND GO GET 'IM!
SMASH!

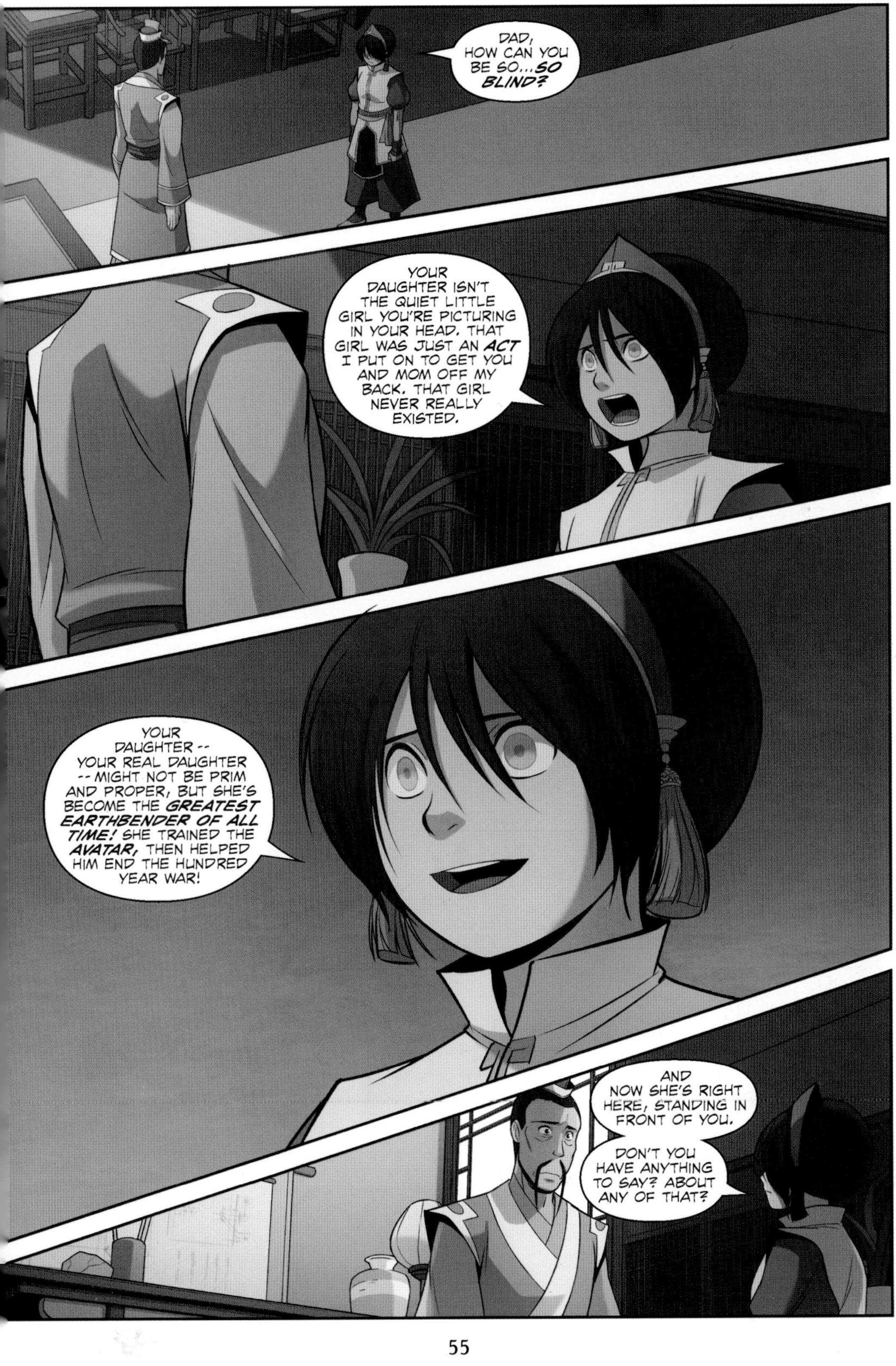
DAD, HOW CAN YOU BE SO... SO BLIND?
YOUR DAUGHTER ISN'T THE QUIET LITTLE GIRL YOU'RE PICTURING IN YOUR HEAD. THAT GIRL WAS JUST AN ACT I PUT ON TO GET YOU AND MOM OFF MY BACK. THAT GIRL NEVER REALLY EXISTED.
YOUR DAUGHTER -- YOUR REAL DAUGHTER -- MIGHT NOT BE PRIM AND PROPER, BUT SHE'S BECOME THE GREATEST EARTHBENDER OF ALL TIME! SHE TRAINED THE AVATAR, THEN HELPED HIM END THE HUNDRED YEAR WAR!
AND NOW SHE'S RIGHT HERE, STANDING IN FRONT OF YOU.
DON'T YOU HAVE ANYTHING TO SAY? ABOUT ANY OF THAT?

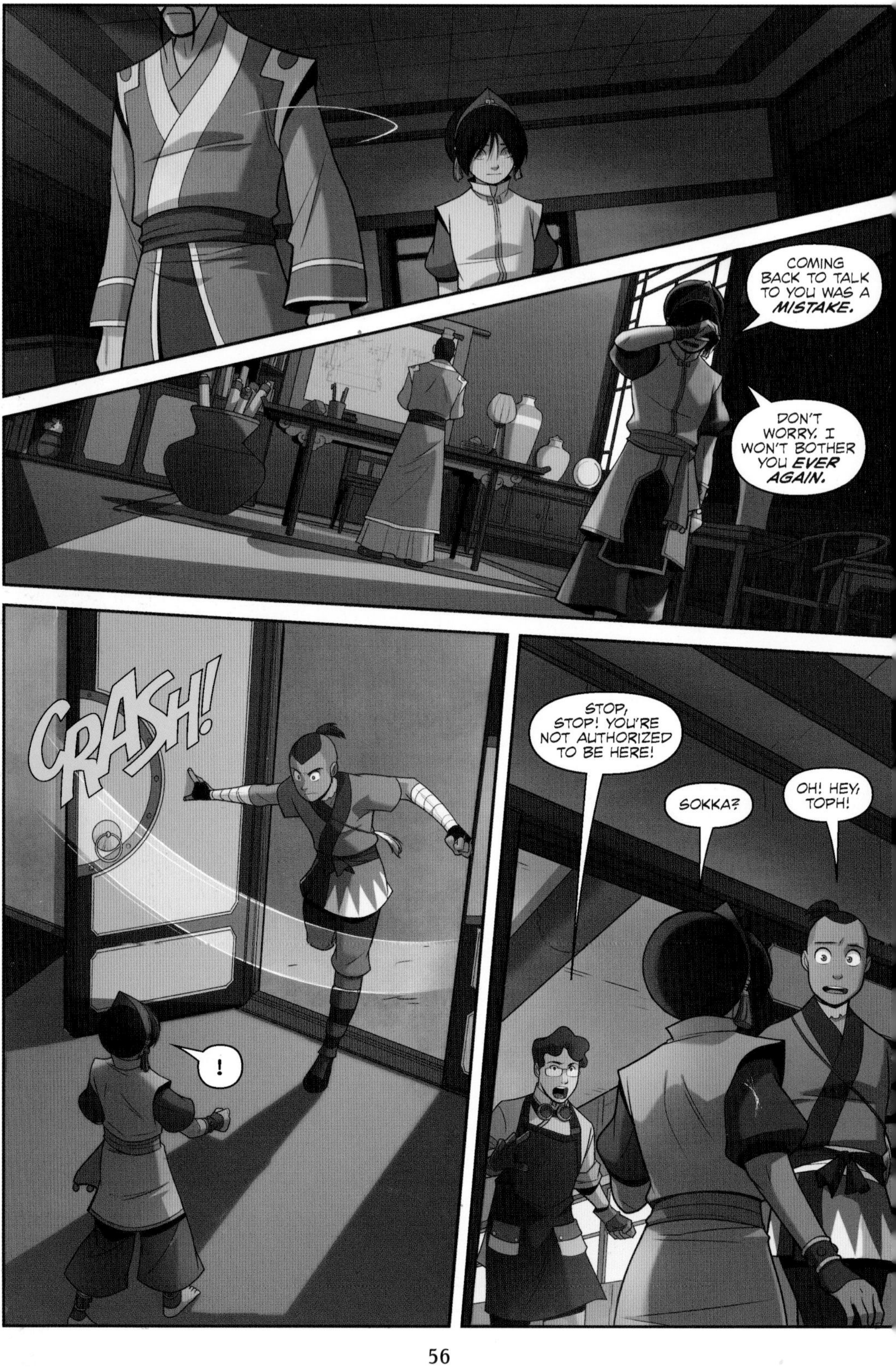
COMING BACK TO TALK TO YOU WAS A *MISTAKE.*
DON'T WORRY. I WON'T BOTHER YOU *EVER AGAIN.*
CRASH!
!
STOP, STOP! YOU'RE NOT AUTHORIZED TO BE HERE!
SOKKA?
OH! HEY, TOPH!

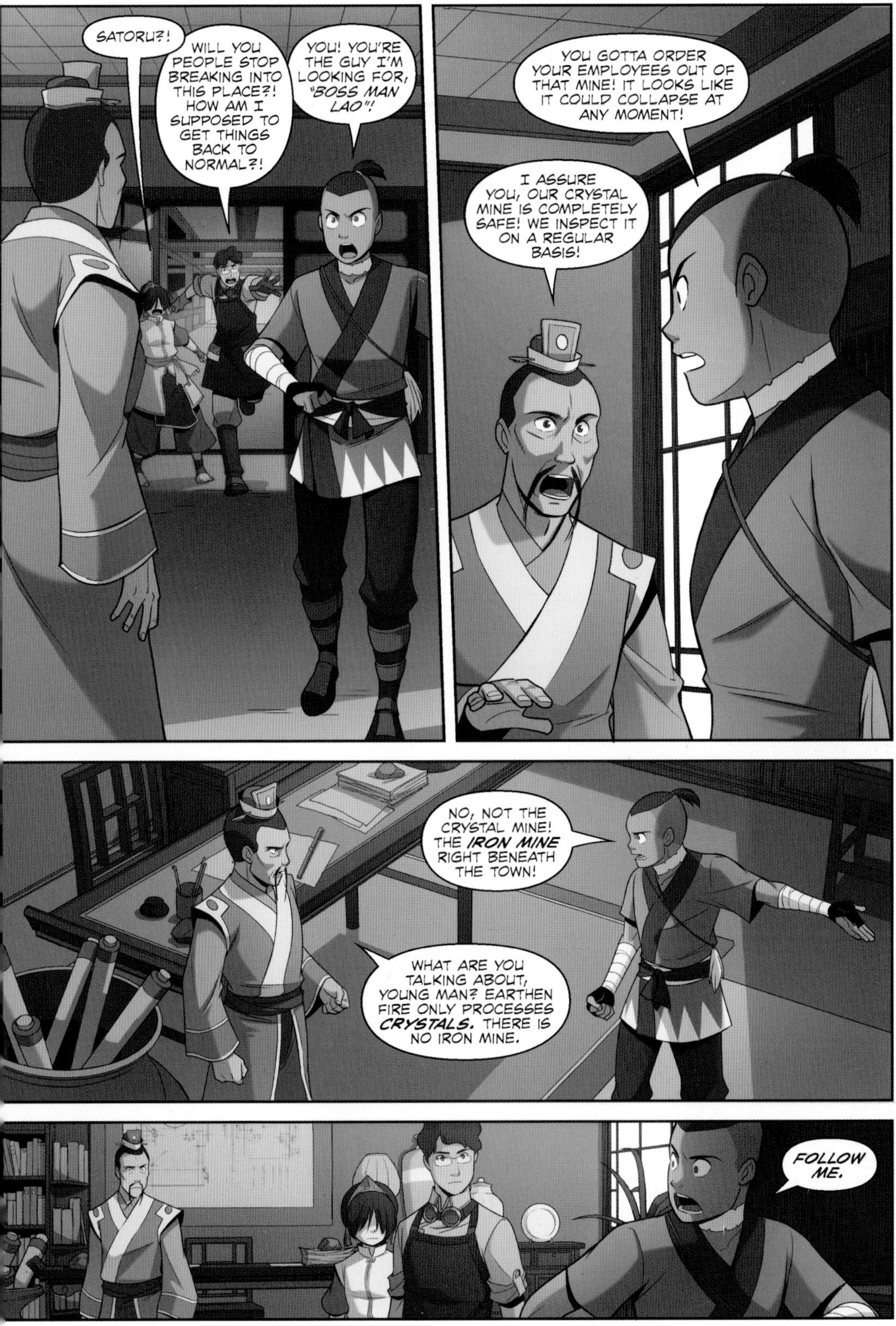
SATORU?!
WILL YOU PEOPLE STOP BREAKING INTO THIS PLACE?! HOW AM I SUPPOSED TO GET THINGS BACK TO NORMAL?!
YOU! YOU'RE THE GUY I'M LOOKING FOR, "BOSS MAN LAO"!
YOU GOTTA ORDER YOUR EMPLOYEES OUT OF THAT MINE! IT LOOKS LIKE IT COULD COLLAPSE AT ANY MOMENT!
I ASSURE YOU, OUR CRYSTAL MINE IS COMPLETELY SAFE! WE INSPECT IT ON A REGULAR BASIS!
NO, NOT THE CRYSTAL MINE! THE IRON MINE RIGHT BENEATH THE TOWN!
WHAT ARE YOU TALKING ABOUT, YOUNG MAN? EARTHEN FIRE ONLY PROCESSES CRYSTALS. THERE IS NO IRON MINE.
FOLLOW ME.

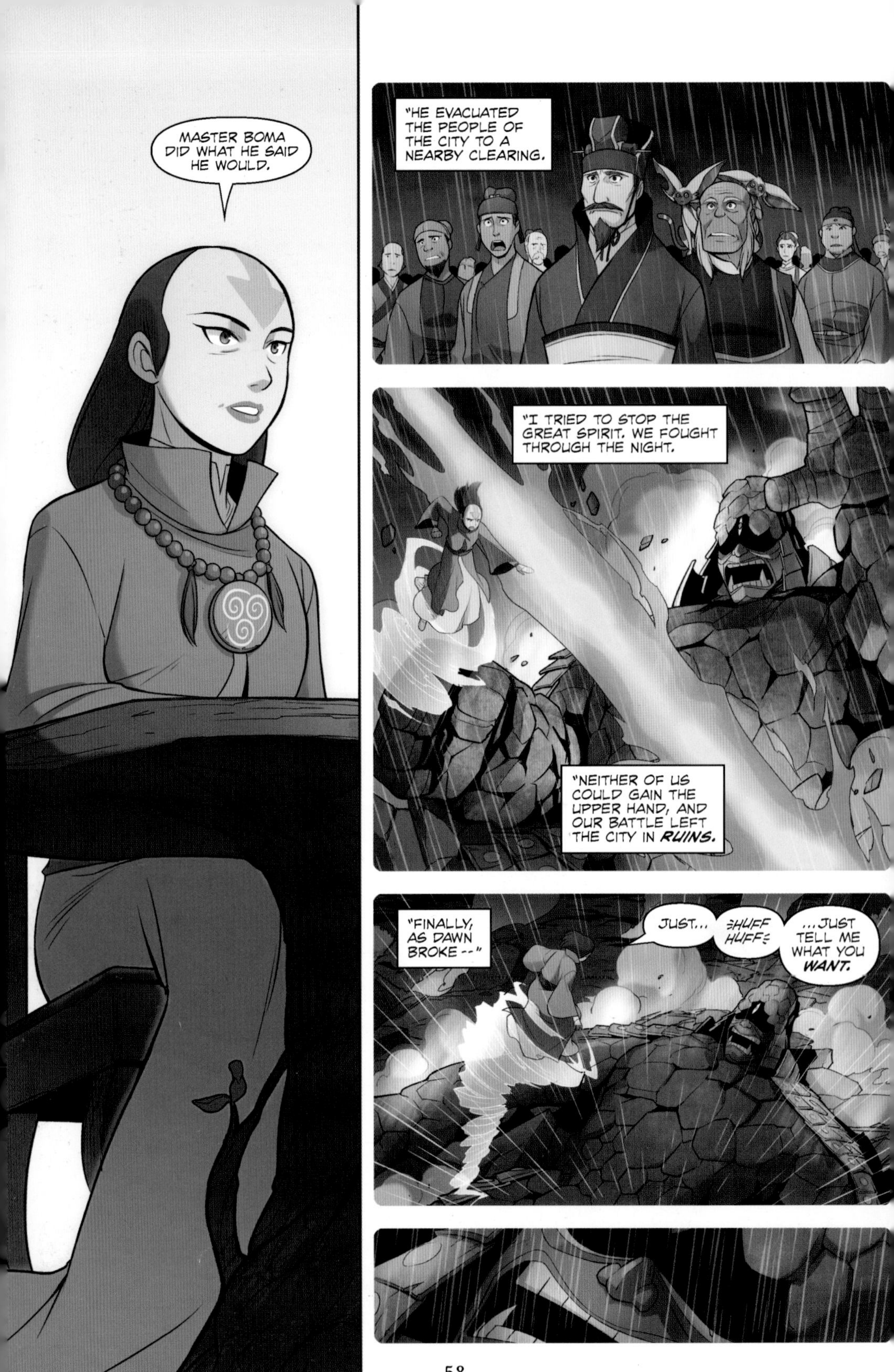
MASTER BOMA DID WHAT HE SAID HE WOULD.
"HE EVACUATED THE PEOPLE OF THE CITY TO A NEARBY CLEARING.
"I TRIED TO STOP THE GREAT SPIRIT. WE FOUGHT THROUGH THE NIGHT.
"NEITHER OF US COULD GAIN THE UPPER HAND, AND OUR BATTLE LEFT THE CITY IN *RUINS.*
"FINALLY, AS DAWN BROKE --"
JUST...
HUFF HUFF
...JUST TELL ME WHAT YOU *WANT.*

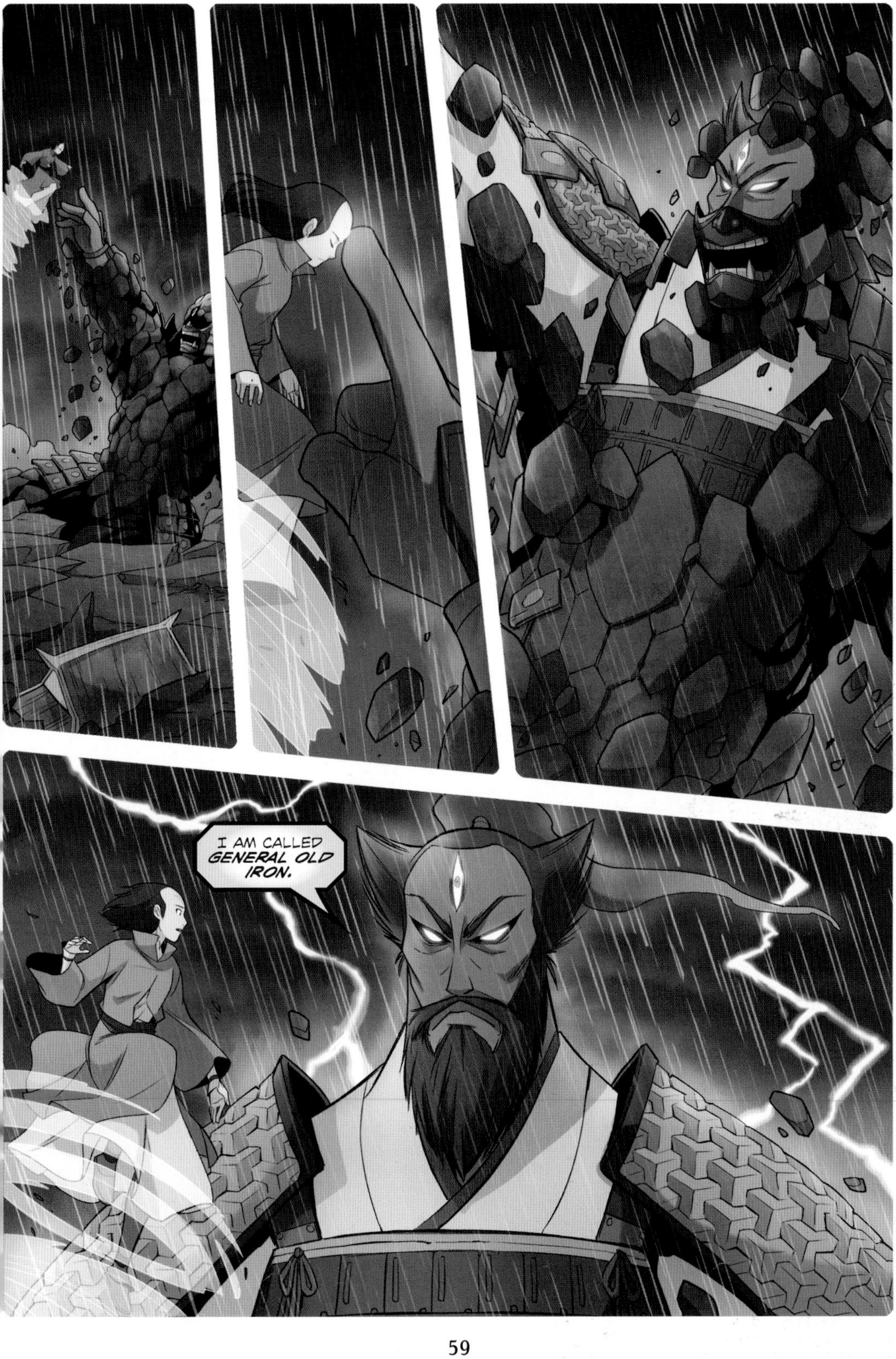
I AM CALLED GENERAL OLD IRON.

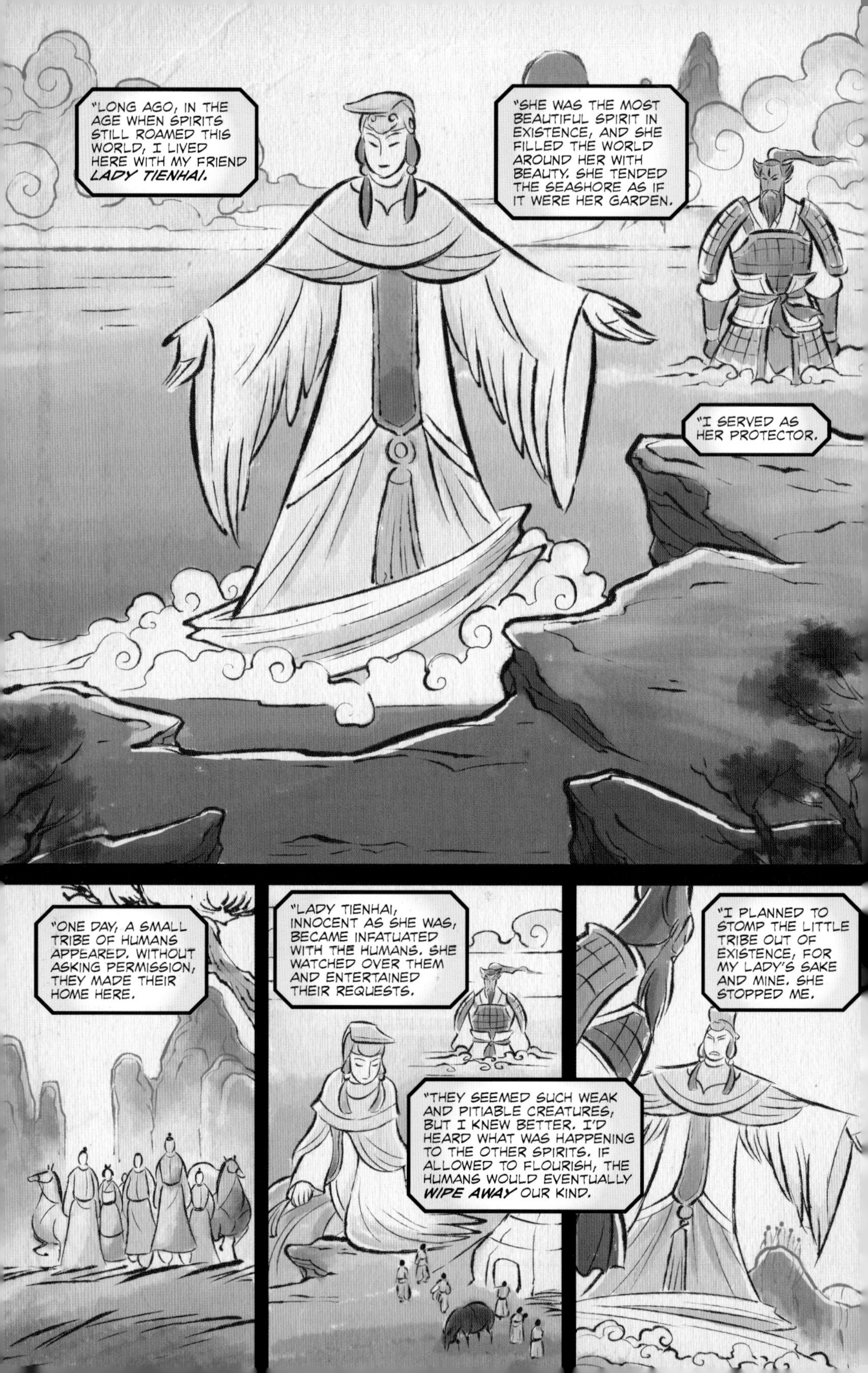
"LONG AGO, IN THE AGE WHEN SPIRITS STILL ROAMED THIS WORLD, I LIVED HERE WITH MY FRIEND *LADY TIENHAI*.
"SHE WAS THE MOST BEAUTIFUL SPIRIT IN EXISTENCE, AND SHE FILLED THE WORLD AROUND HER WITH BEAUTY. SHE TENDED THE SEASHORE AS IF IT WERE HER GARDEN.
"I SERVED AS HER PROTECTOR.
"ONE DAY, A SMALL TRIBE OF HUMANS APPEARED. WITHOUT ASKING PERMISSION, THEY MADE THEIR HOME HERE.
"LADY TIENHAI, INNOCENT AS SHE WAS, BECAME INFATUATED WITH THE HUMANS. SHE WATCHED OVER THEM AND ENTERTAINED THEIR REQUESTS.
"THEY SEEMED SUCH WEAK AND PITIABLE CREATURES, BUT I KNEW BETTER. I'D HEARD WHAT WAS HAPPENING TO THE OTHER SPIRITS. IF ALLOWED TO FLOURISH, THE HUMANS WOULD EVENTUALLY *WIPE AWAY* OUR KIND.
"I PLANNED TO STOMP THE LITTLE TRIBE OUT OF EXISTENCE, FOR MY LADY'S SAKE AND MINE. SHE STOPPED ME.

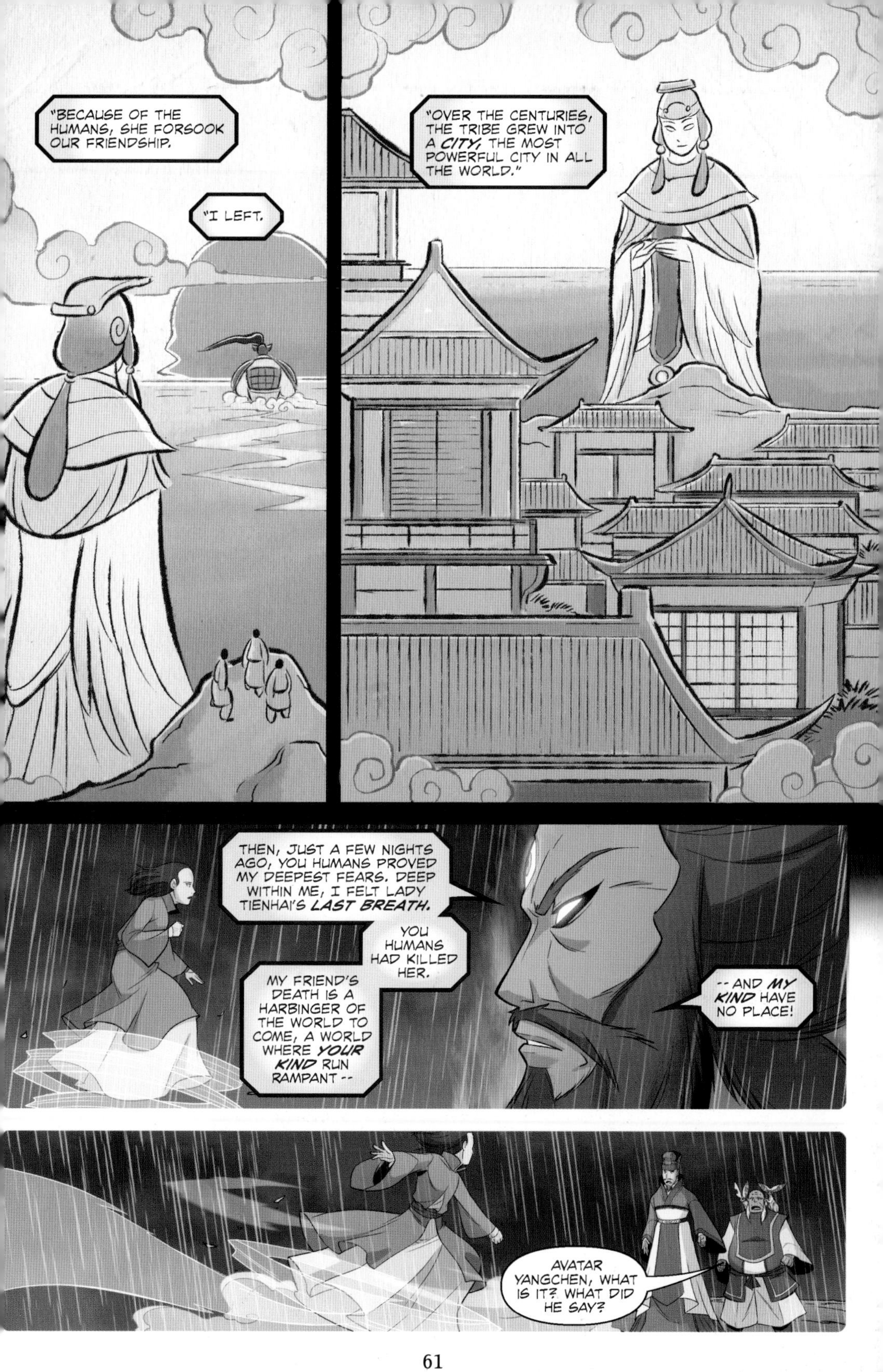
"BECAUSE OF THE HUMANS, SHE FORSOOK OUR FRIENDSHIP.
"I LEFT.
"OVER THE CENTURIES, THE TRIBE GREW INTO A CITY, THE MOST POWERFUL CITY IN ALL THE WORLD."
THEN, JUST A FEW NIGHTS AGO, YOU HUMANS PROVED MY DEEPEST FEARS. DEEP WITHIN ME, I FELT LADY TIENHAI'S LAST BREATH.
YOU HUMANS HAD KILLED HER.
MY FRIEND'S DEATH IS A HARBINGER OF THE WORLD TO COME, A WORLD WHERE YOUR KIND RUN RAMPANT --
-- AND MY KIND HAVE NO PLACE!
AVATAR YANGCHEN, WHAT IS IT? WHAT DID HE SAY?

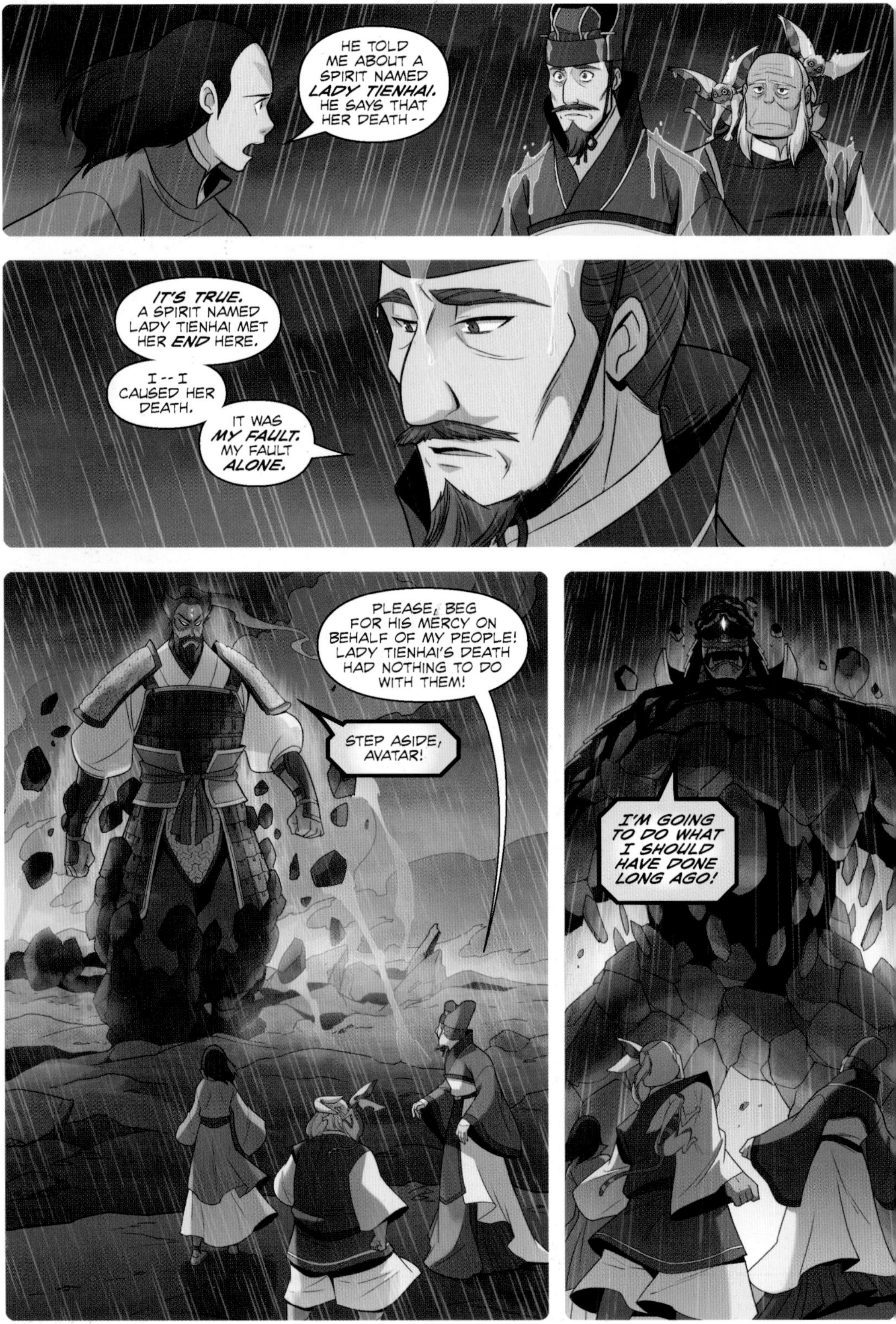
HE TOLD ME ABOUT A SPIRIT NAMED LADY TIENHAI. HE SAYS THAT HER DEATH --
IT'S TRUE. A SPIRIT NAMED LADY TIENHAI MET HER END HERE.
I -- I CAUSED HER DEATH.
IT WAS MY FAULT. MY FAULT ALONE.
PLEASE, BEG FOR HIS MERCY ON BEHALF OF MY PEOPLE! LADY TIENHAI'S DEATH HAD NOTHING TO DO WITH THEM!
STEP ASIDE, AVATAR!
I'M GOING TO DO WHAT I SHOULD HAVE DONE LONG AGO!

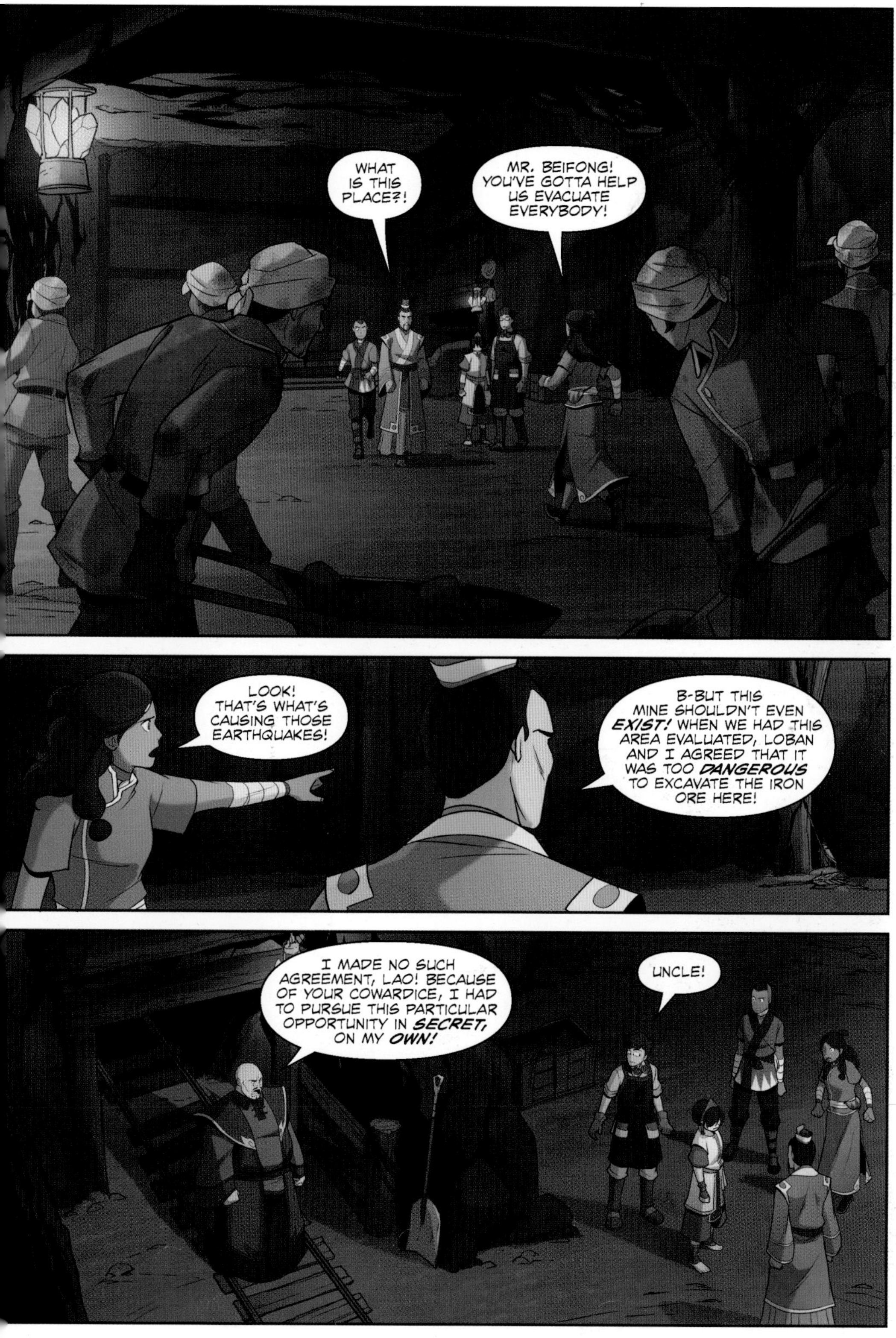
WHAT IS THIS PLACE?!
MR. BEIFONG! YOU'VE GOTTA HELP US EVACUATE EVERYBODY!
LOOK! THAT'S WHAT'S CAUSING THOSE EARTHQUAKES!
B-BUT THIS MINE SHOULDN'T EVEN EXIST! WHEN WE HAD THIS AREA EVALUATED, LOBAN AND I AGREED THAT IT WAS TOO DANGEROUS TO EXCAVATE THE IRON ORE HERE!
I MADE NO SUCH AGREEMENT, LAO! BECAUSE OF YOUR COWARDICE, I HAD TO PURSUE THIS PARTICULAR OPPORTUNITY IN SECRET, ON MY OWN!
UNCLE!

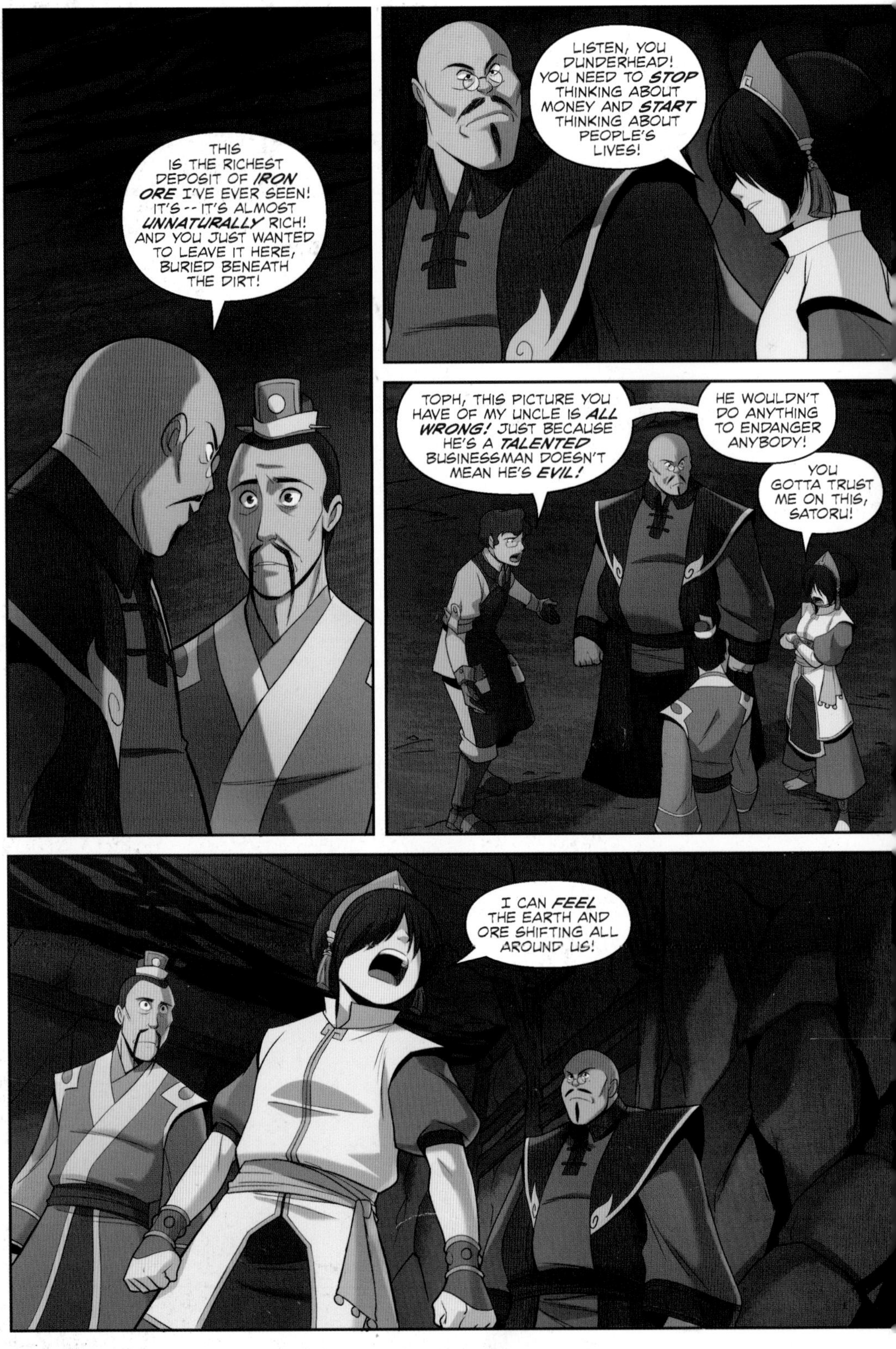
THIS IS THE RICHEST DEPOSIT OF IRON ORE I'VE EVER SEEN! IT'S -- IT'S ALMOST UNNATURALLY RICH! AND YOU JUST WANTED TO LEAVE IT HERE, BURIED BENEATH THE DIRT!
LISTEN, YOU DUNDERHEAD! YOU NEED TO STOP THINKING ABOUT MONEY AND START THINKING ABOUT PEOPLE'S LIVES!
TOPH, THIS PICTURE YOU HAVE OF MY UNCLE IS ALL WRONG! JUST BECAUSE HE'S A TALENTED BUSINESSMAN DOESN'T MEAN HE'S EVIL!
HE WOULDN'T DO ANYTHING TO ENDANGER ANYBODY!
YOU GOTTA TRUST ME ON THIS, SATORU!
I CAN FEEL THE EARTH AND ORE SHIFTING ALL AROUND US!

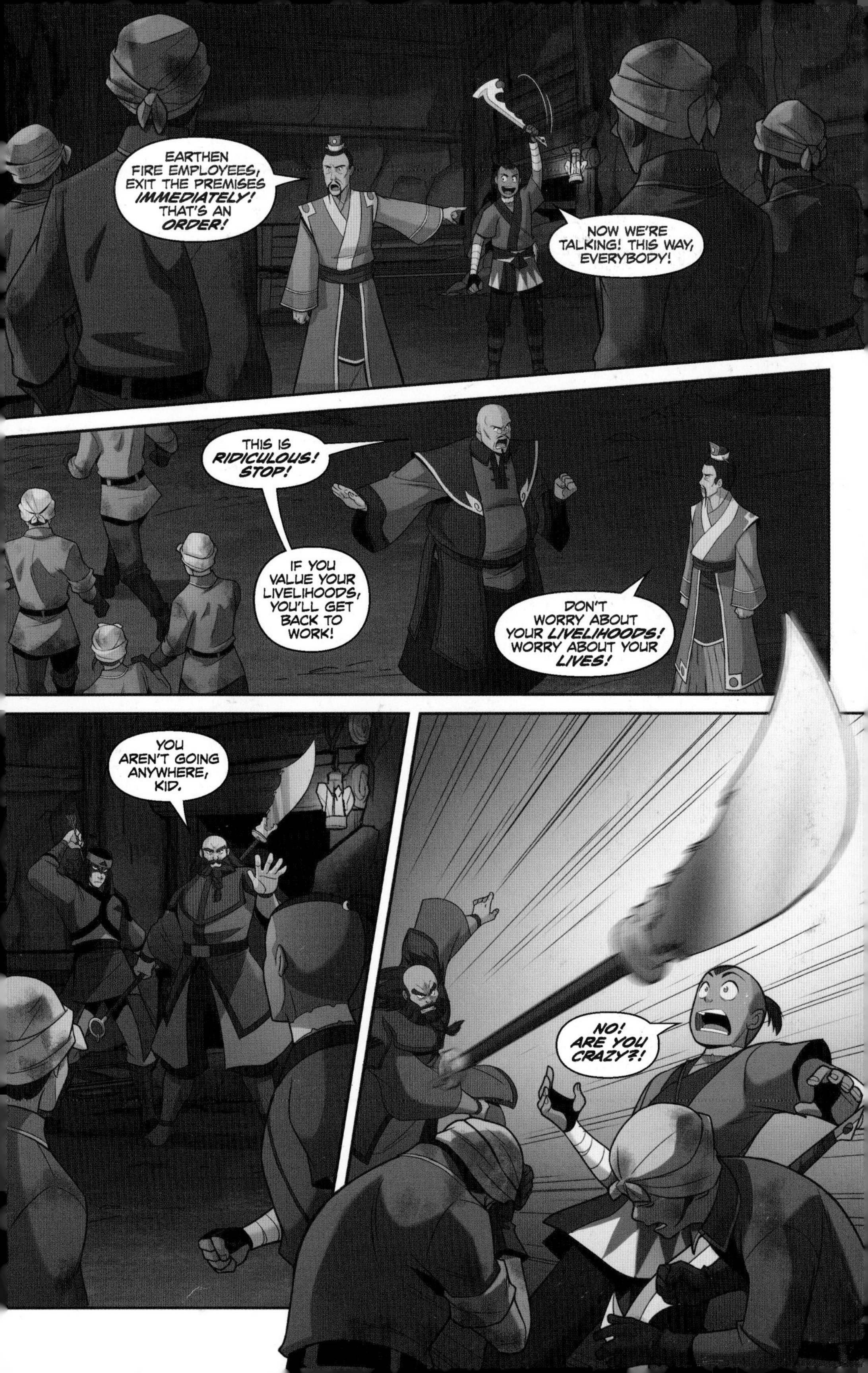
EARTHEN FIRE EMPLOYEES, EXIT THE PREMISES IMMEDIATELY! THAT'S AN ORDER!
NOW WE'RE TALKING! THIS WAY, EVERYBODY!
THIS IS RIDICULOUS! STOP!
IF YOU VALUE YOUR LIVELIHOODS, YOU'LL GET BACK TO WORK!
DON'T WORRY ABOUT YOUR LIVELIHOODS! WORRY ABOUT YOUR LIVES!
YOU AREN'T GOING ANYWHERE, KID.
NO! ARE YOU CRAZY?!

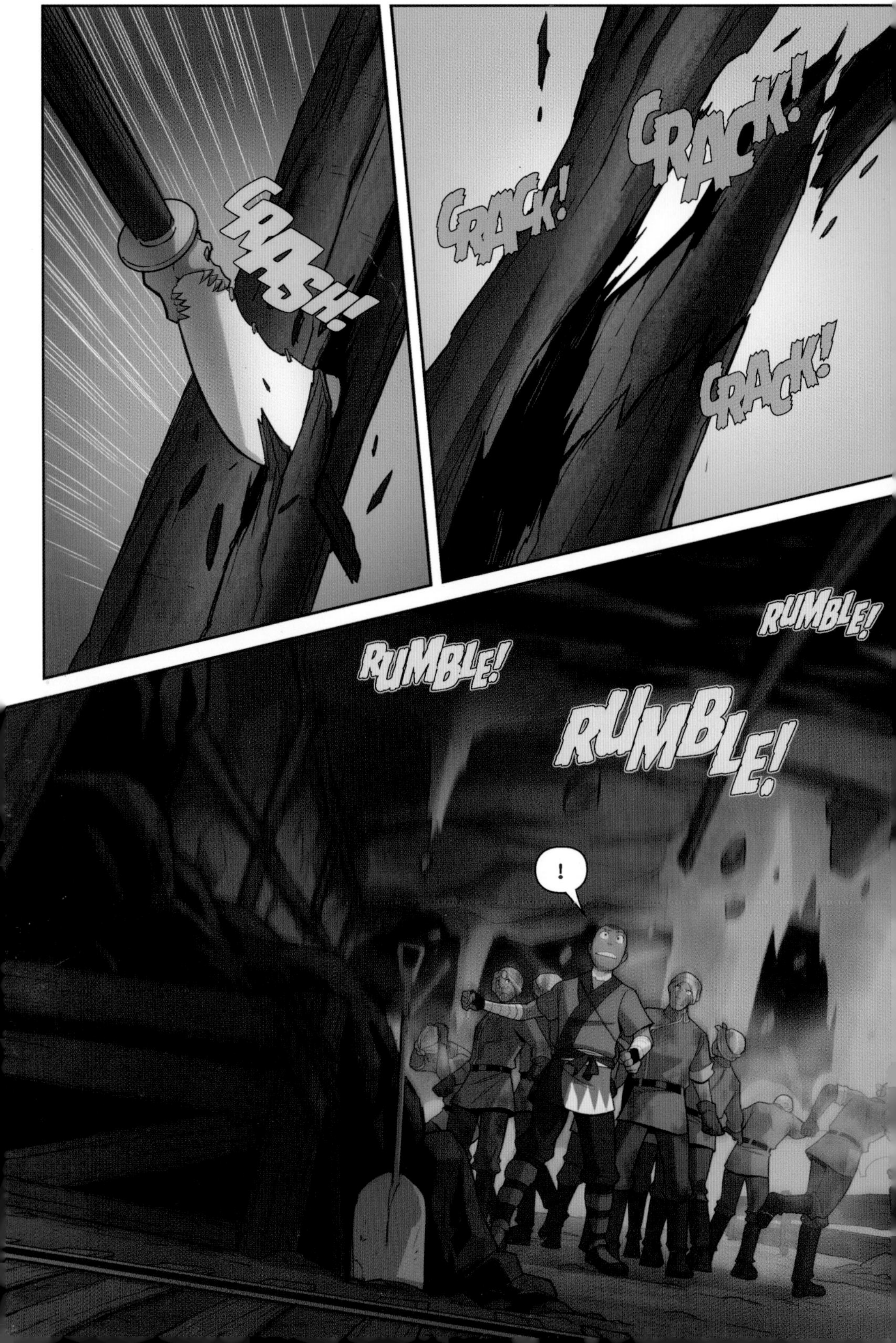
CRASH!
CRACK!
CRACK!
CRACK!
RUMBLE!
RUMBLE!
RUMBLE!
!

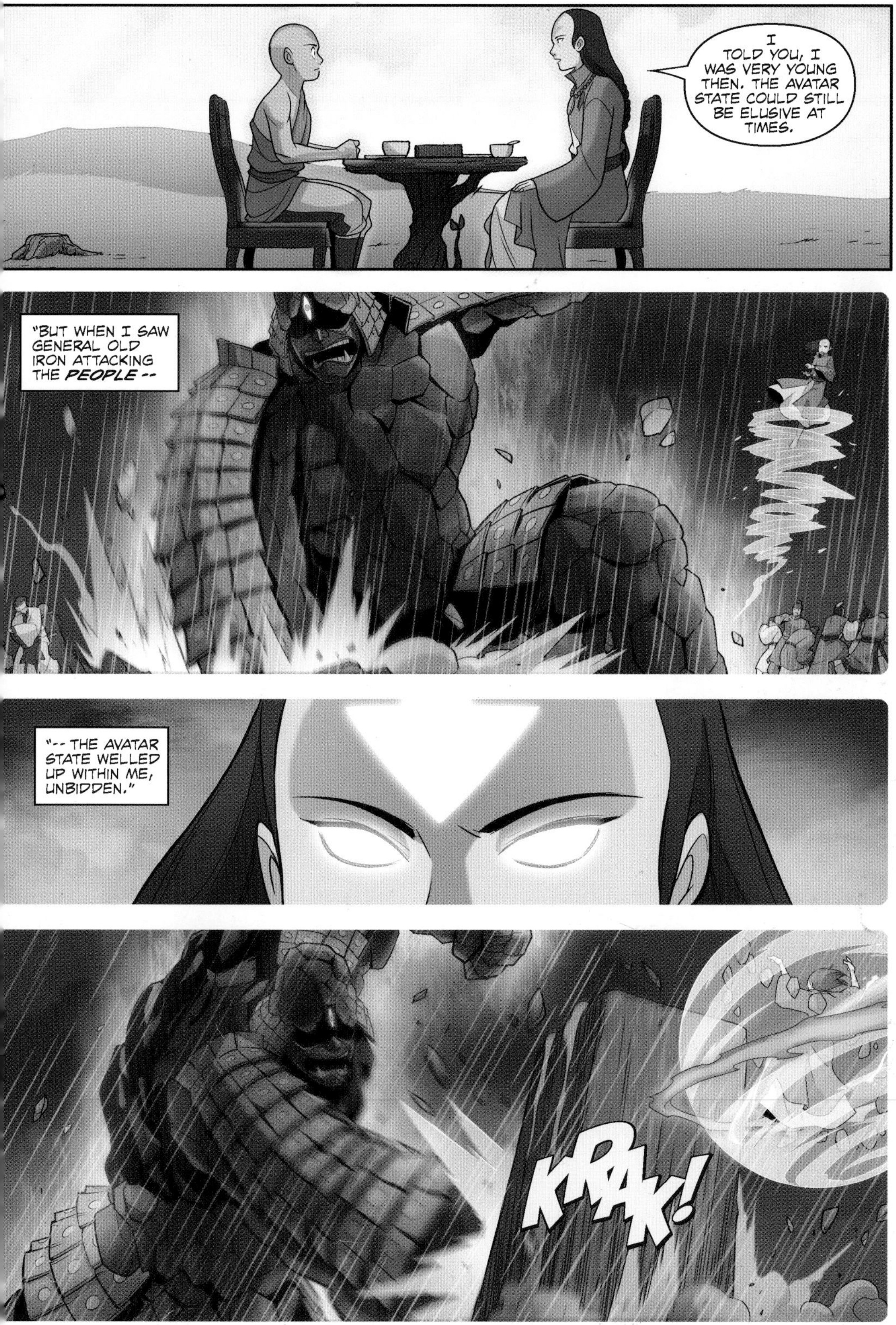
I TOLD YOU, I WAS VERY YOUNG THEN. THE AVATAR STATE COULD STILL BE ELUSIVE AT TIMES.
"BUT WHEN I SAW GENERAL OLD IRON ATTACKING THE *PEOPLE* --
"-- THE AVATAR STATE WELLED UP WITHIN ME, UNBIDDEN."
KRAK!

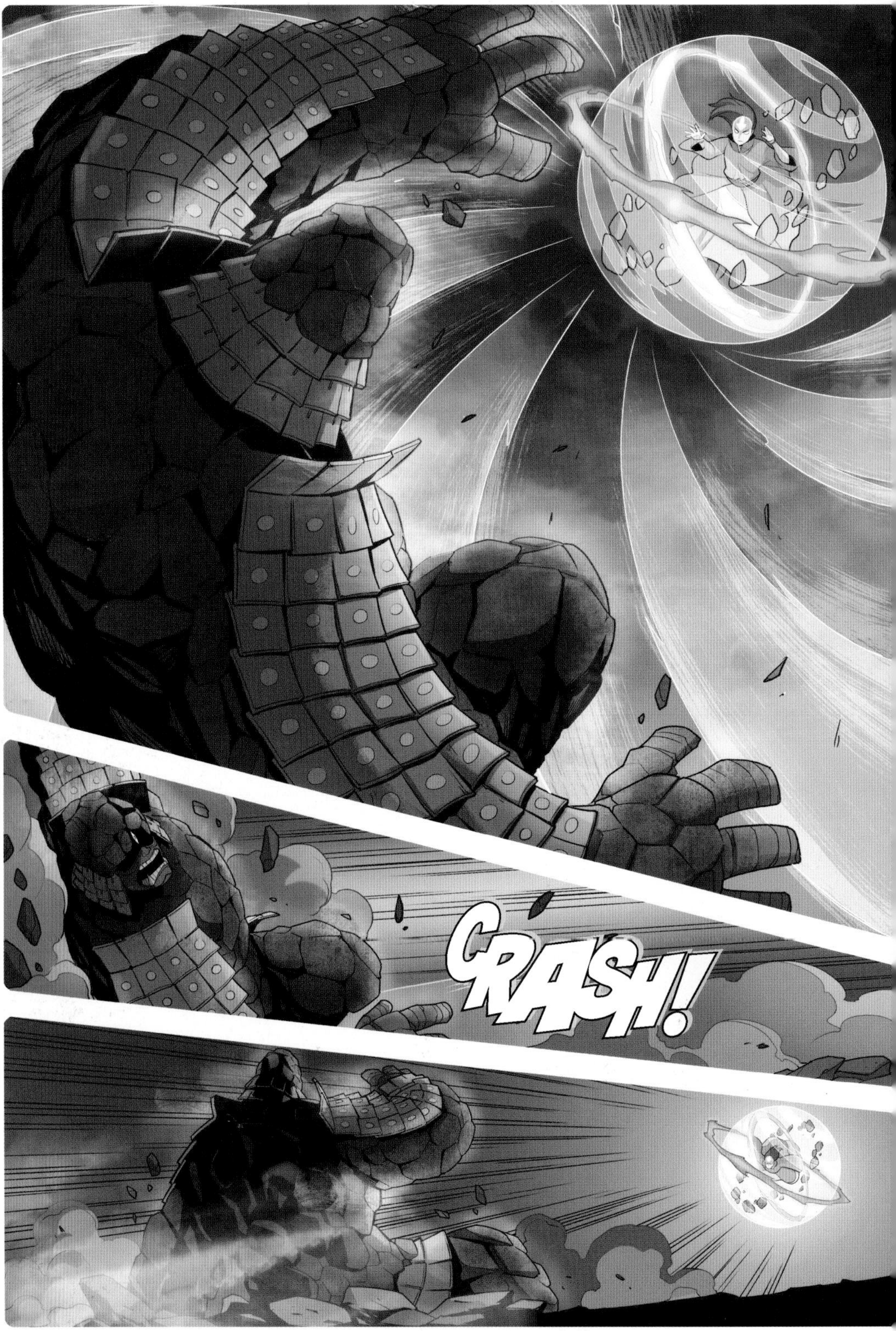
CRASH!

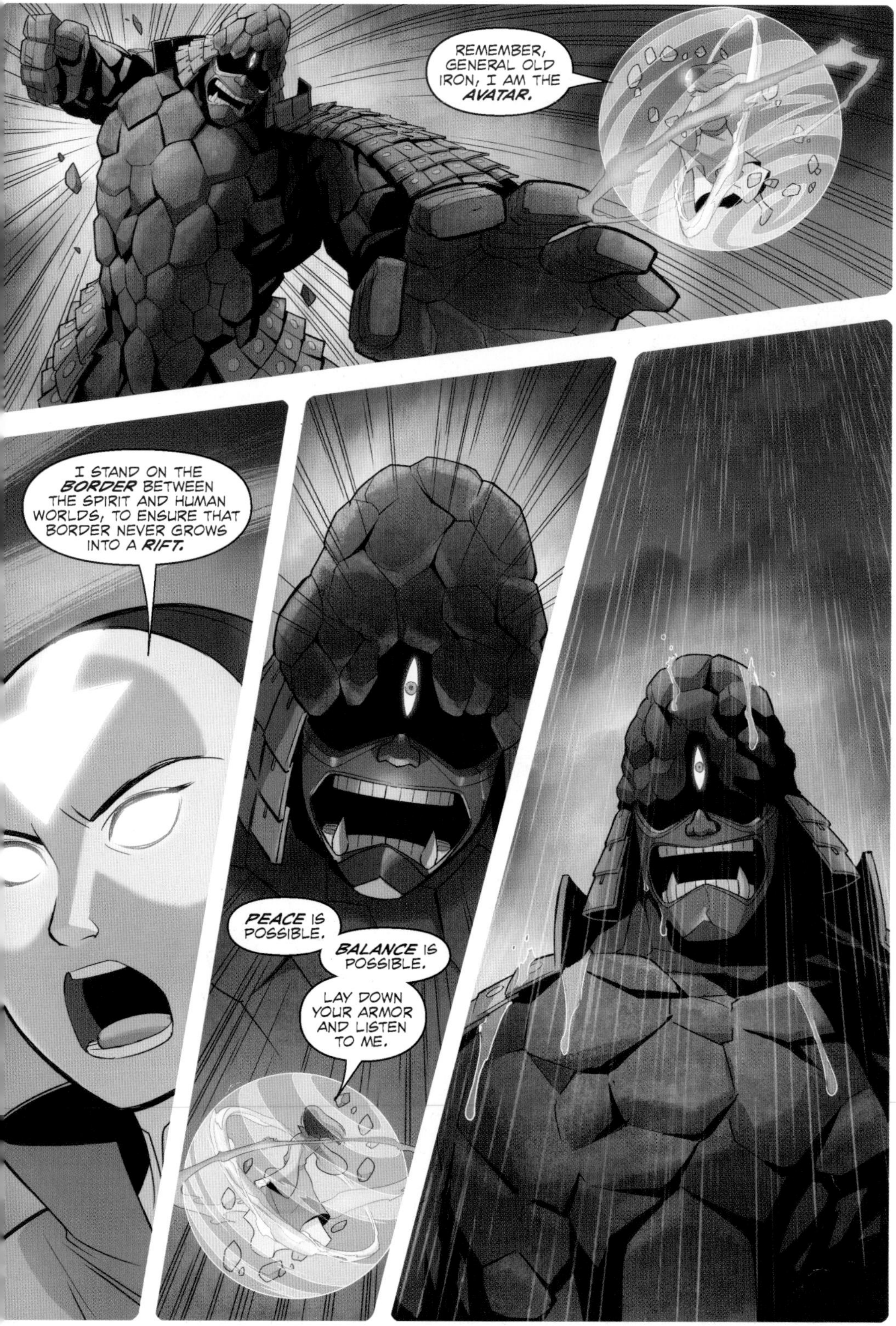

REMEMBER, GENERAL OLD IRON, I AM THE AVATAR.
I STAND ON THE BORDER BETWEEN THE SPIRIT AND HUMAN WORLDS, TO ENSURE THAT BORDER NEVER GROWS INTO A RIFT.
PEACE IS POSSIBLE.
BALANCE IS POSSIBLE.
LAY DOWN YOUR ARMOR AND LISTEN TO ME.

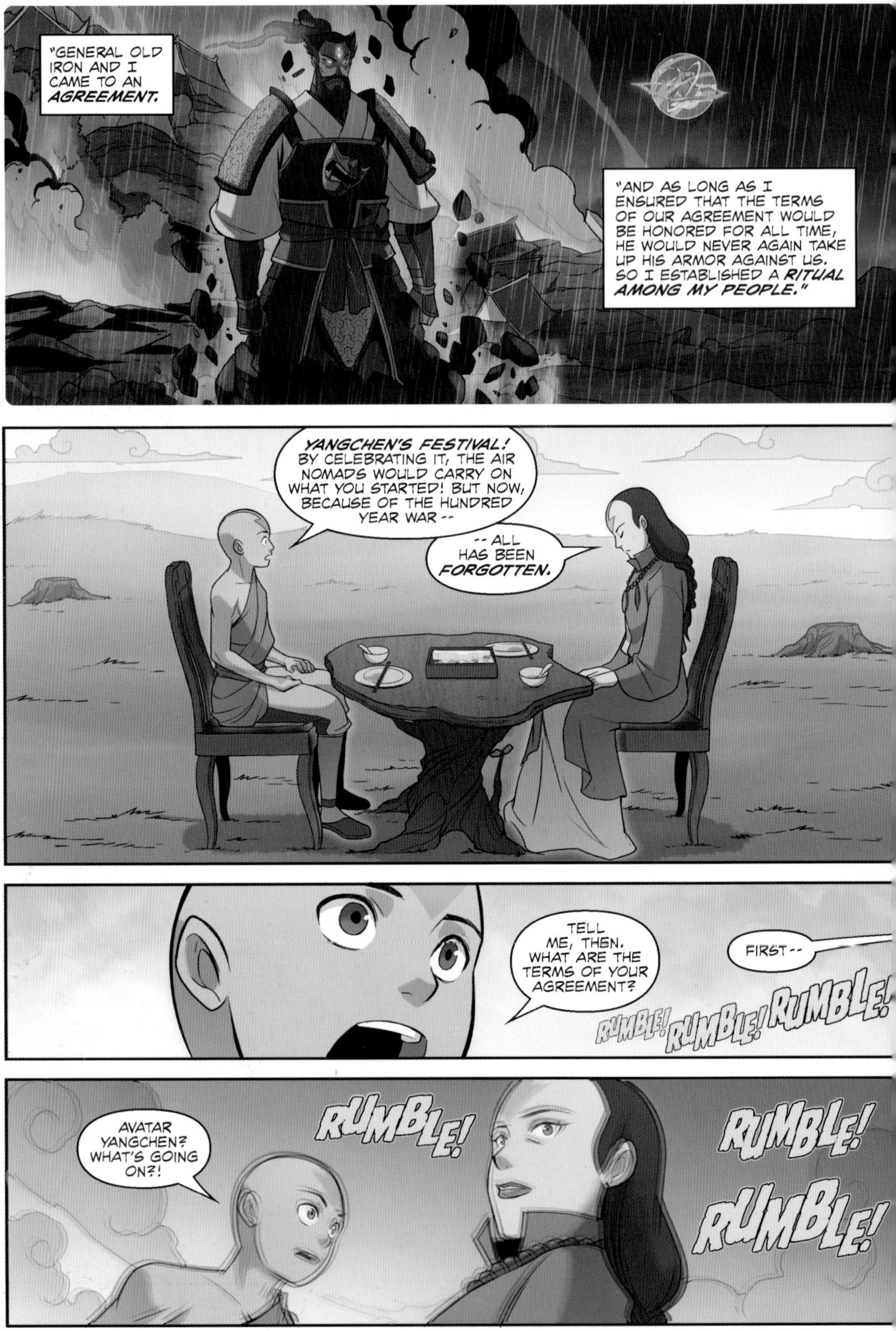
"GENERAL OLD IRON AND I CAME TO AN *AGREEMENT.*
"AND AS LONG AS I ENSURED THAT THE TERMS OF OUR AGREEMENT WOULD BE HONORED FOR ALL TIME, HE WOULD NEVER AGAIN TAKE UP HIS ARMOR AGAINST US. SO I ESTABLISHED A *RITUAL AMONG MY PEOPLE."*
YANGCHEN'S FESTIVAL! BY CELEBRATING IT, THE AIR NOMADS WOULD CARRY ON WHAT YOU STARTED! BUT NOW, BECAUSE OF THE HUNDRED YEAR WAR --
-- ALL HAS BEEN *FORGOTTEN.*
TELL ME, THEN. WHAT ARE THE TERMS OF YOUR AGREEMENT?
FIRST --
RUMBLE! RUMBLE! RUMBLE!
AVATAR YANGCHEN? WHAT'S GOING ON?!
RUMBLE!
RUMBLE!
RUMBLE!

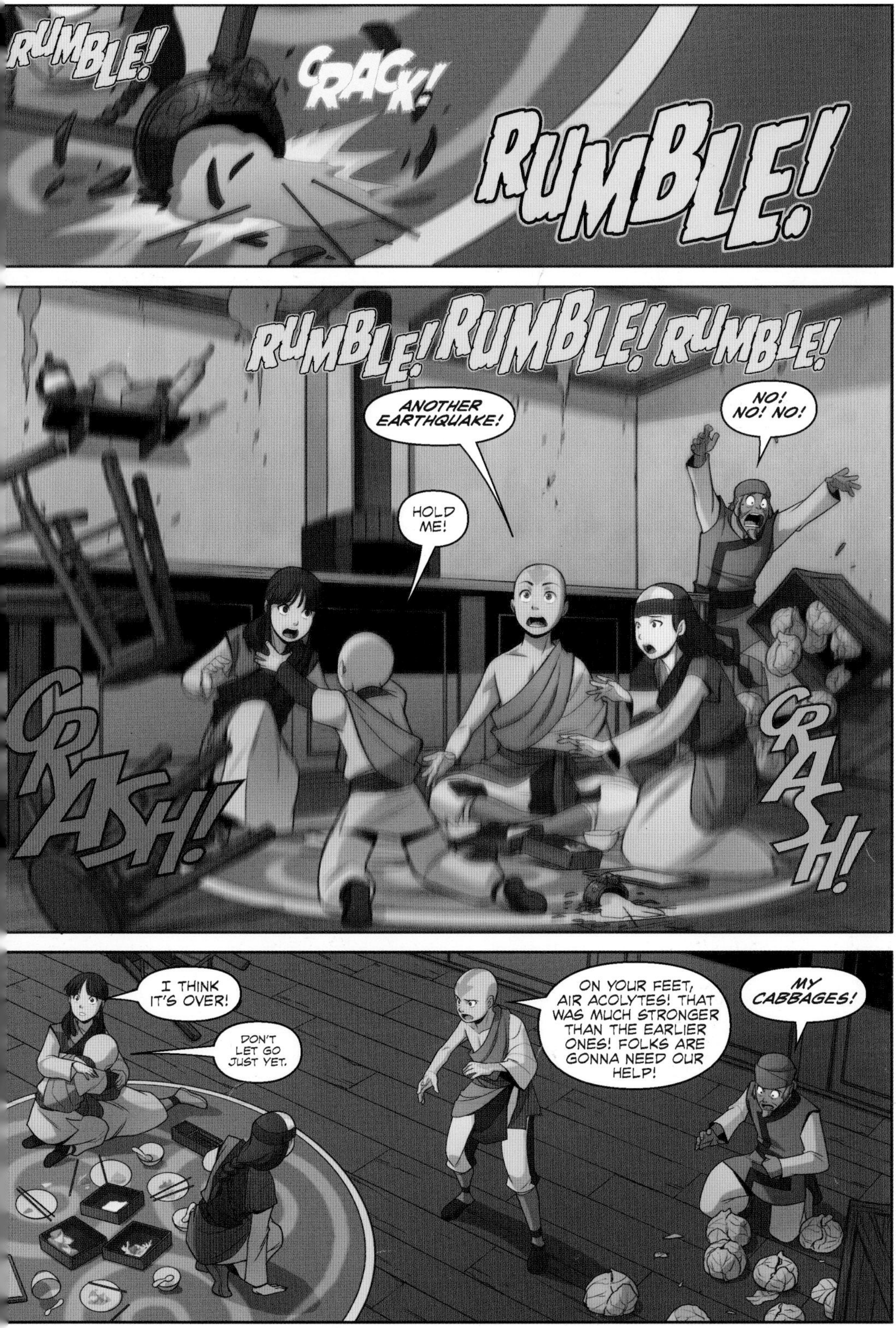
RUMBLE!
CRACK!
RUMBLE!
RUMBLE! RUMBLE! RUMBLE!
ANOTHER EARTHQUAKE!
NO! NO! NO!
HOLD ME!
CRASH!
CRASH!
I THINK IT'S OVER!
DON'T LET GO JUST YET.
ON YOUR FEET, AIR ACOLYTES! THAT WAS MUCH STRONGER THAN THE EARLIER ONES! FOLKS ARE GONNA NEED OUR HELP!
MY CABBAGES!

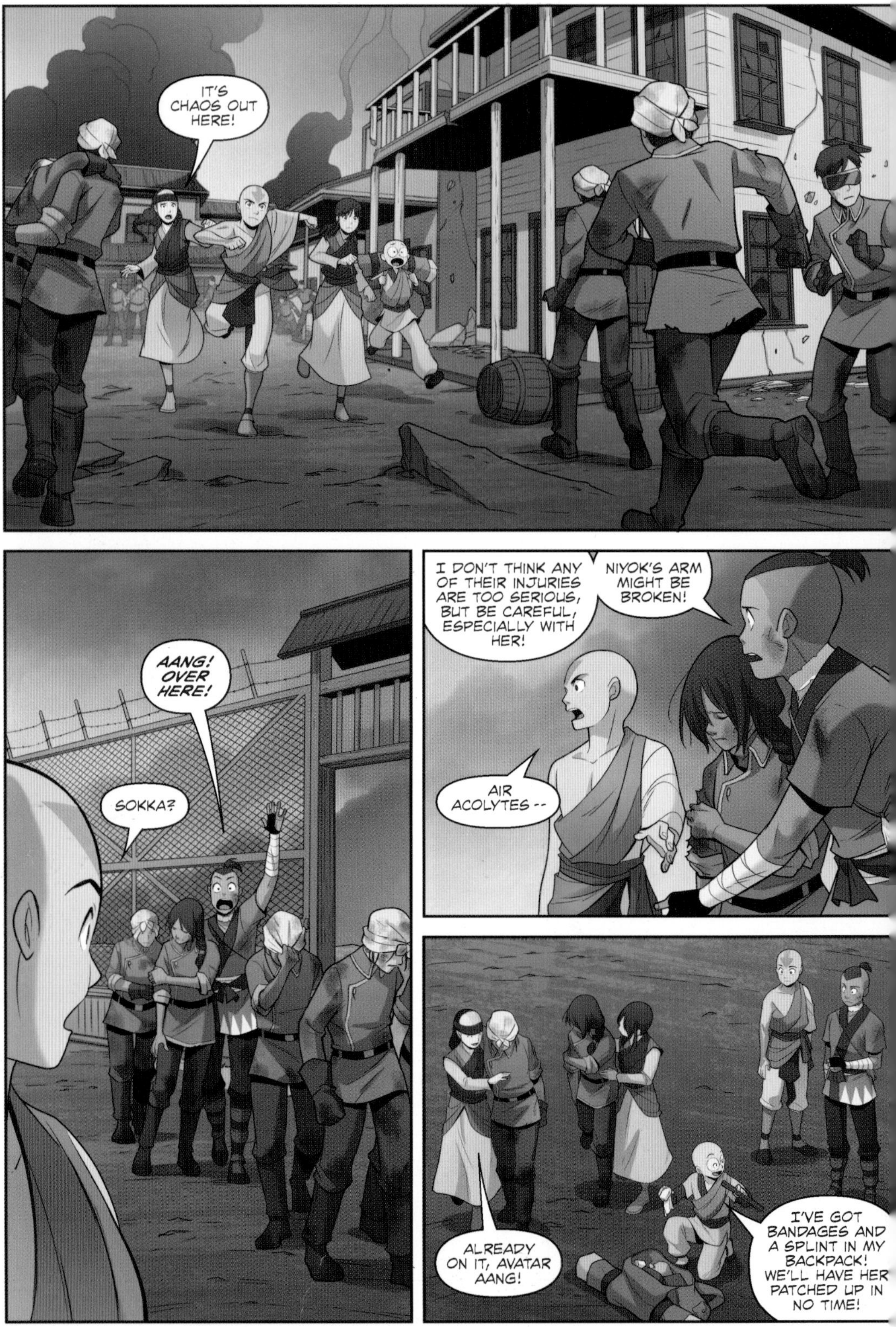
IT'S CHAOS OUT HERE!
AANG! OVER HERE!
SOKKA?
I DON'T THINK ANY OF THEIR INJURIES ARE TOO SERIOUS, BUT BE CAREFUL, ESPECIALLY WITH HER!
NIYOK'S ARM MIGHT BE BROKEN!
AIR ACOLYTES --
ALREADY ON IT, AVATAR AANG!
I'VE GOT BANDAGES AND A SPLINT IN MY BACKPACK! WE'LL HAVE HER PATCHED UP IN NO TIME!

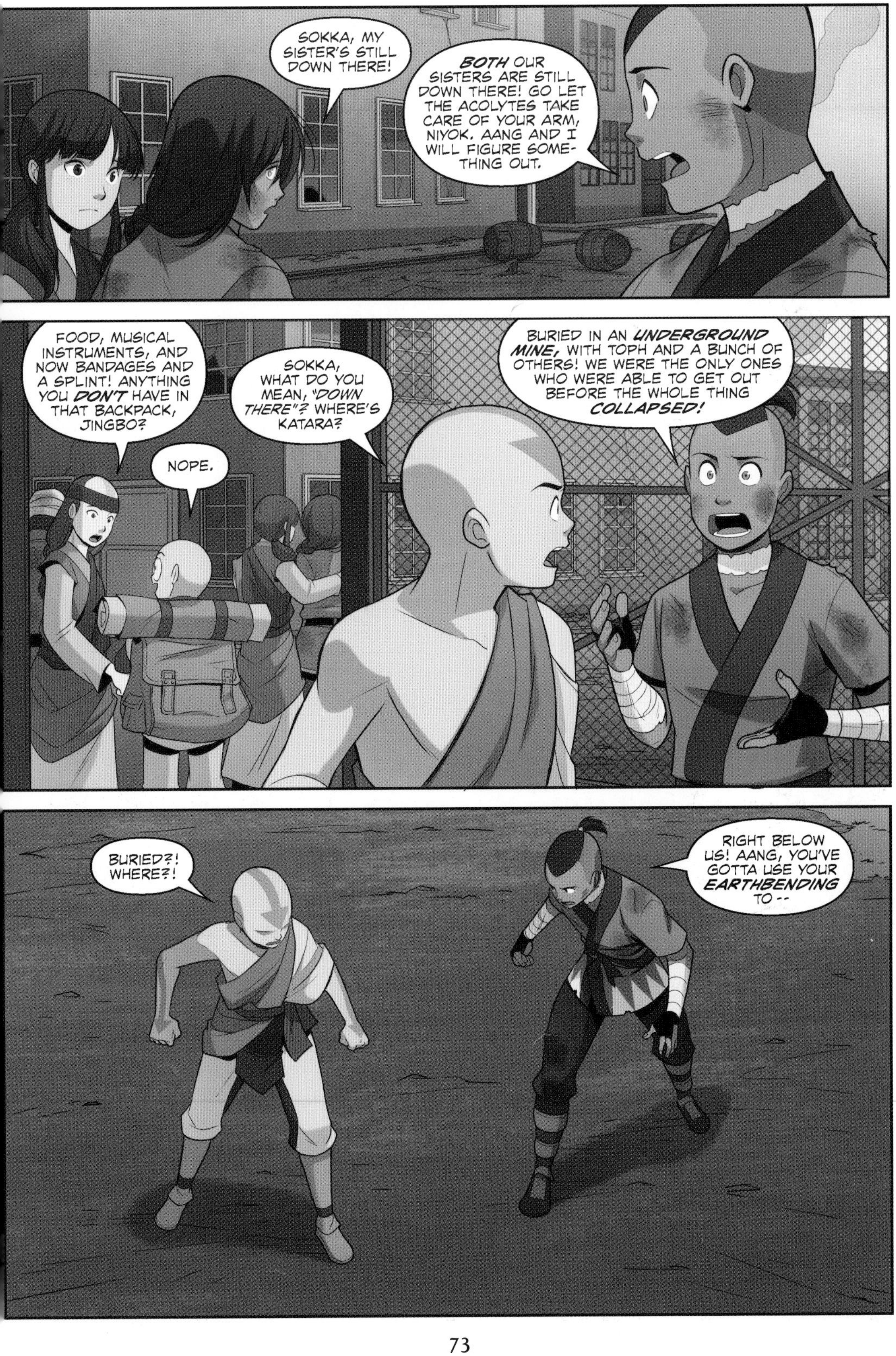
SOKKA, MY SISTER'S STILL DOWN THERE!
BOTH OUR SISTERS ARE STILL DOWN THERE! GO LET THE ACOLYTES TAKE CARE OF YOUR ARM, NIYOK. AANG AND I WILL FIGURE SOME-THING OUT.
FOOD, MUSICAL INSTRUMENTS, AND NOW BANDAGES AND A SPLINT! ANYTHING YOU DON'T HAVE IN THAT BACKPACK, JINGBO?
NOPE.
SOKKA, WHAT DO YOU MEAN, "DOWN THERE"? WHERE'S KATARA?
BURIED IN AN UNDERGROUND MINE, WITH TOPH AND A BUNCH OF OTHERS! WE WERE THE ONLY ONES WHO WERE ABLE TO GET OUT BEFORE THE WHOLE THING COLLAPSED!
BURIED?! WHERE?!
RIGHT BELOW US! AANG, YOU'VE GOTTA USE YOUR EARTHBENDING TO --

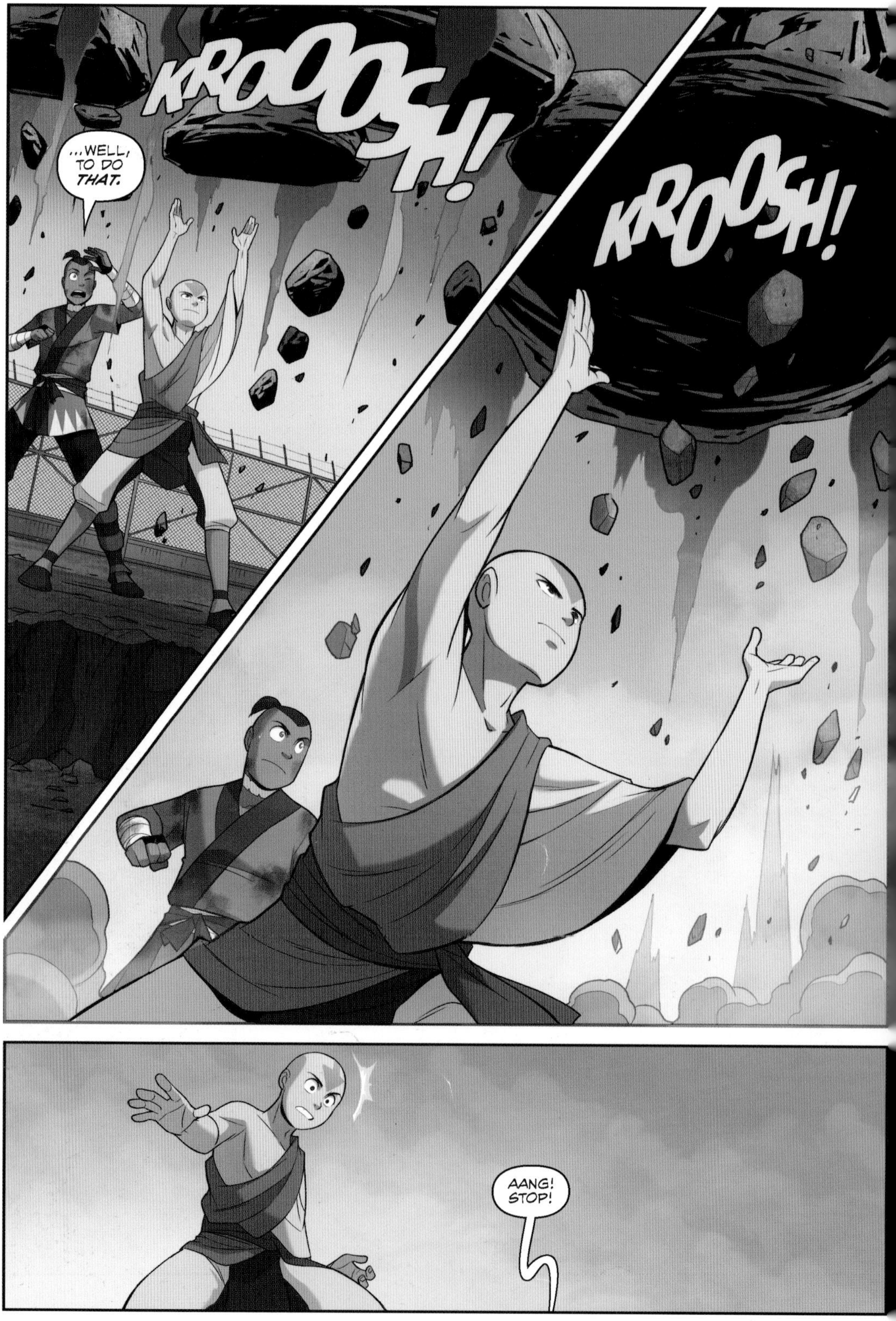
KROOOSH!
...WELL, TO DO THAT.
KROOSH!
AANG! STOP!

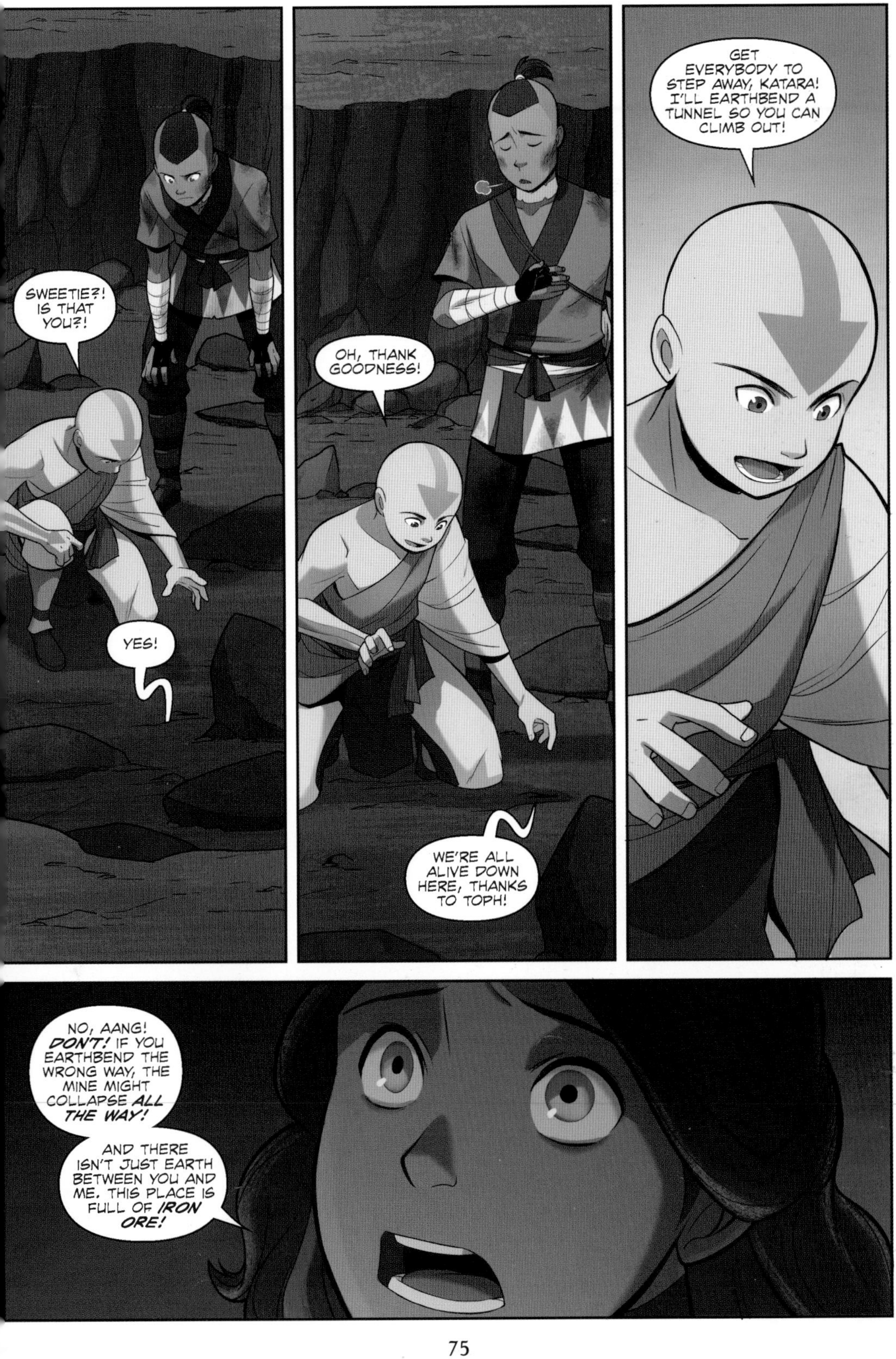
SWEETIE?! IS THAT YOU?!
YES!
OH, THANK GOODNESS!
WE'RE ALL ALIVE DOWN HERE, THANKS TO TOPH!
GET EVERYBODY TO STEP AWAY, KATARA! I'LL EARTHBEND A TUNNEL SO YOU CAN CLIMB OUT!
NO, AANG! *DON'T!* IF YOU EARTHBEND THE WRONG WAY, THE MINE MIGHT COLLAPSE *ALL THE WAY!*
AND THERE ISN'T JUST EARTH BETWEEN YOU AND ME. THIS PLACE IS FULL OF *IRON ORE!*

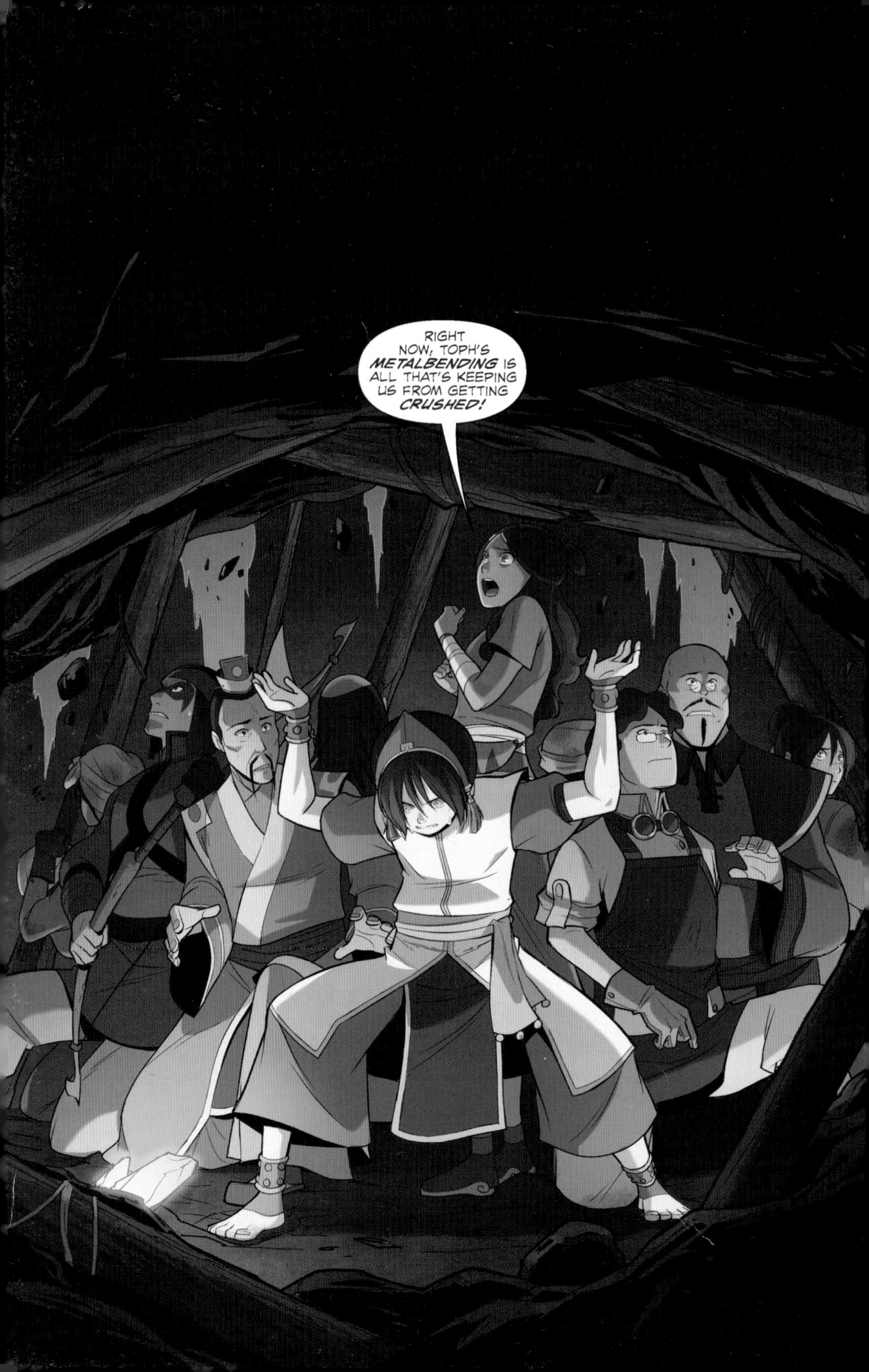
RIGHT NOW, TOPH'S METALBENDING IS ALL THAT'S KEEPING US FROM GETTING CRUSHED!

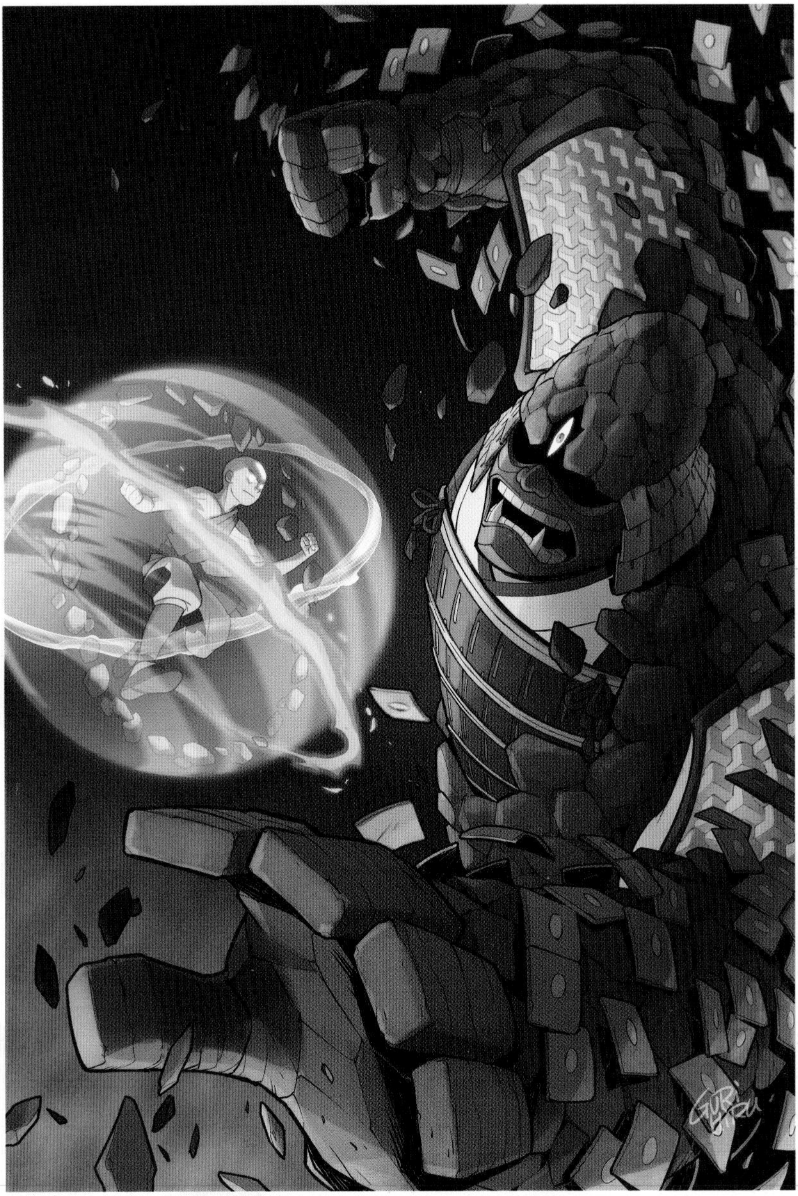

COMING IN NOVEMBER

Aang must make peace between spirits and humans in . . .

THE RIFT • PART THREE

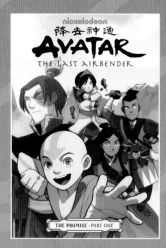

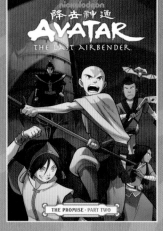

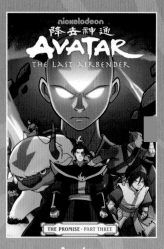

nickelodeon
AVATAR
THE LAST AIRBENDER
THE PROMISE · PART ONE

Avatar:
The Last Airbender—
The Promise Part 1

978-1-59582-811-8 | $10.99

nickelodeon
AVATAR
THE LAST AIRBENDER
THE PROMISE · PART TWO

Avatar:
The Last Airbender—
The Promise Part 2

978-1-59582-875-0 | $10.99

nickelodeon
AVATAR
THE LAST AIRBENDER
THE PROMISE · PART THREE

Avatar:
The Last Airbender—
The Promise Part 3

978-1-59582-941-2 | $10.99

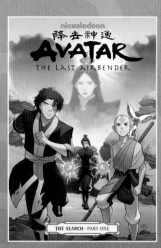

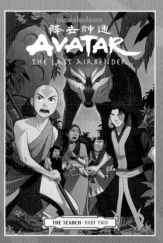

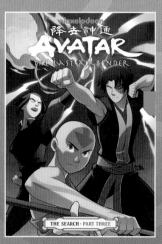

nickelodeon
AVATAR
THE LAST AIRBENDER
THE SEARCH · PART ONE

Avatar:
The Last Airbender—
The Search Part 1

978-1-61655-054-7 | $10.99

nickelodeon
AVATAR
THE LAST AIRBENDER
THE SEARCH · PART TWO

Avatar:
The Last Airbender—
The Search Part 2

978-1-61655-190-2 | $10.99

nickelodeon
AVATAR
THE LAST AIRBENDER
THE SEARCH · PART THREE

Avatar:
The Last Airbender—
The Search Part 3

978-1-61655-184-1 | $10.99

BOOK ONE: AIR
THE ART OF THE ANIMATED SERIE

An exclusive look behind the scenes of this acclaimed television series! Featuring hundreds of never-before-seen images, including storyboards, character designs, and location paintings, all with commentary from the creators of the show!

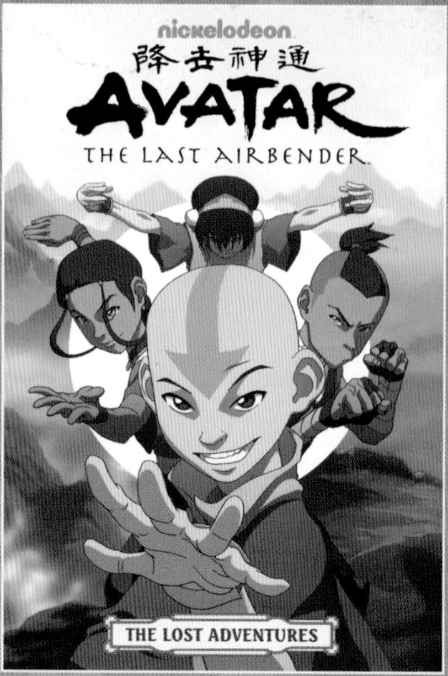
nickelodeon
AVATAR
THE LAST AIRBENDER
THE LOST ADVENTURES

Avatar: The Last Airbender—
The Lost Adventures

978-1-59582-748-7 | $14.99

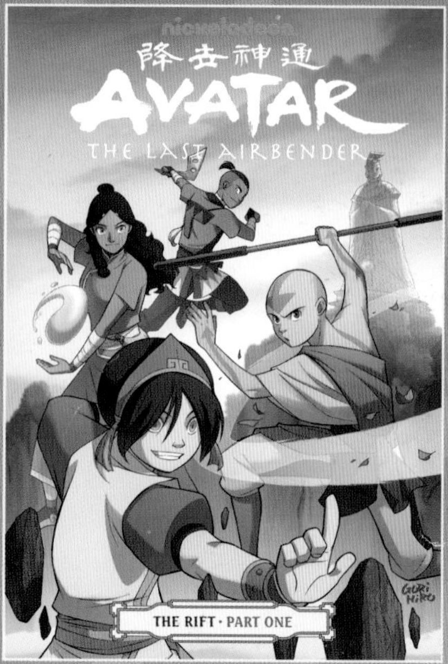
AVATAR
THE LAST AIRBENDER
THE RIFT · PART ONE

Avatar: The Last Airbender—
The Rift Part 1

978-1-61655-295-4 | $10.99

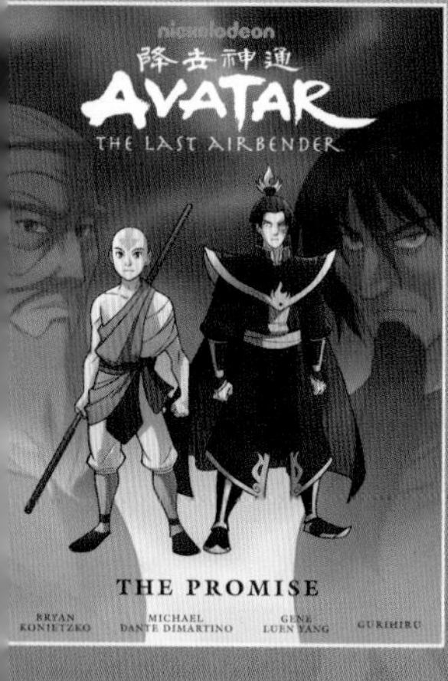
nickelodeon
AVATAR
THE LAST AIRBENDER
THE PROMISE
BRYAN KONIETZKO
MICHAEL DANTE DIMARTINO
GENE LUEN YANG
GURIHIRU

Avatar:
The Last Airbender—
he Promise Library Edition

78-1-61655-074-5 | $39.99

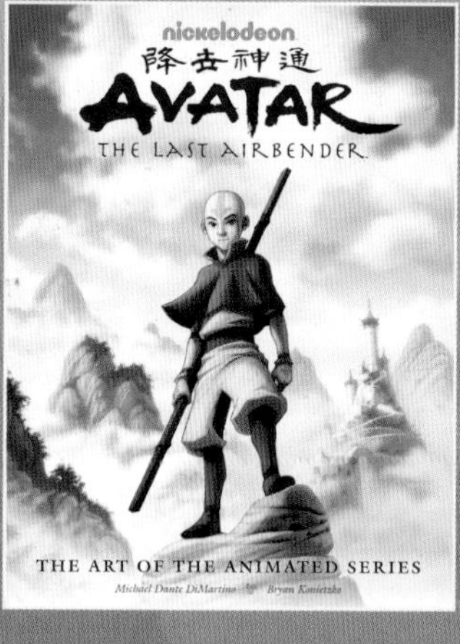
nickelodeon
AVATAR
THE LAST AIRBENDER
THE ART OF THE ANIMATED SERIES
Michael Dante DiMartino
Bryan Konietzko

Avatar:
The Last Airbender—
The Art of the Animated Series

978-1-59582-504-9 | $34.99

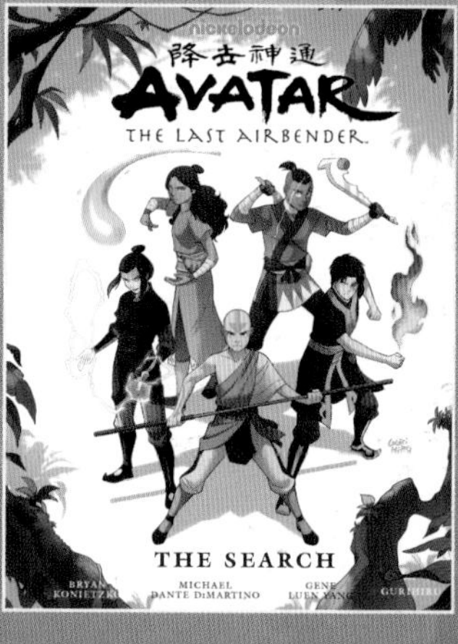
nickelodeon
AVATAR
THE LAST AIRBENDER
THE SEARCH
MICHAEL DANTE DIMARTINO

Avatar:
The Last Airbender—
The Search Library Edition

978-1-61655-226-8 | $39.99

AVAILABLE AT YOUR LOCAL COMICS SHOP OR BOOKSTORE.

To find a comics shop in your area, call 1-888-266-4226

For more information or to order direct, visit DarkHorse.com or call 1-800-862-0052

DARK HORSE BOOKS

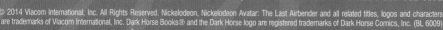